Medical Sociology

Medical sociology:

a general systems approach

Leon S. Robertson, Ph.D.
Margaret C. Heagarty, M.D.

nh Nelson-Hall Publishers·Chicago

Library of Congress Cataloging in Publication Data

Robertson, Leon S
    Medical sociology

    Bibliography: p.
    Includes indexes
    1. Social medicine.   I.   Heagarty, Margaret C.,
joint author.   II.   Title.   [DNLM: 1.   Social medicine.   WA30 R651m]
RA418.R58   362.1   75-9779
ISBN 0-88229-127-0

Manufactured in the United States of America

Contents

Preface

This is a textbook in medical sociology. The book is intended primarily for advanced undergraduate students, graduate students in sociology, and for medical students in behavioral science or community medicine courses. It contains some ideas that we have not seen in print and that our colleagues in behavioral science and in medicine may find useful as well.

Many textbooks state principles and theories as facts in a field with little or no qualification. We have chosen to air some dirty linen, both in sociology and in medicine. Graduate students and medical students often complain that they have to "unlearn" some of what they were taught as undergraduates because of the qualifications and uncertainties that accompany the generalizations of any science. We have stated many qualifications and uncertainties, perhaps too many, perhaps not enough. We intend and hope our readers will finish this book motivated to pursue the subject further, either in empirical research or by examining the detailed studies cited in the references.

Although our references are numerous, they are a highly selective sample of what is available in the field. We have not attempted an exhaustive literature review on any issue. Instead, we have chosen topics that are especially relevant to the future health and welfare of the human race, and have cited work illustrative of some of the ideas that are being brought to bear on these issues. In many cases we have been critical of the ideas or research methods. We apologize in advance for any misstatement of an author's ideas or research results. However, we make no apologies for our skeptical view of some of the past research or of some of the current trends in medicine and sociology. Healthy skepticism of the conventional wisdom in any field is a prerequisite for fresh thinking and research. To withhold such skepticism from future professionals in a field is to invite stagnation.

Sociology is the study of human interaction, the social arrangements in human groups, and the consequences for the individuals and groups involved. Medicine is the application of technology and knowledge to the prevention and amelioration of human damage and suffering. For human beings to apply technology and knowledge to other human beings, human interaction and social arrangements are required. It is therefore appropriate that sociologists examine the interaction, social arrangements, and consequences that affect health and illness. Sociologists who engage in such work are called medical sociologists.

The work of medical sociology is hampered by a number of problems. The field of sociology generally is young relative to most other sciences, and, in many cases, the available research tools and methods are primitive. Most sociologists, including medical sociologists, have but a layman's knowledge of medical technology, medical training, and the history of the evolution of medical practice. Access to the people and organizations that could provide or arrange for the collection of appropriate data is often difficult. Some physicians, like many others, are wary of individuals who claim to be able to study human interaction and social arrangements with the same scientific approach as is used to study atoms and cells.

One obvious way to overcome at least some of these problems is for sociologists and physicians to collaborate in research—teaching and learning from one another. Many sociologists are no less wary of such arrangements with physicians than are physicians with sociologists. The fear of being coopted into a defense of conventional wisdom in medicine is real and, in some cases, justified. Each party must enter a collaborative arrangement with respect for the other's unique background and skills, while maintaining the healthy skepticism appropriate to any scientist.

We have been fortunate as sociologist (Dr. Robertson) and physician (Dr. Heagarty) to have collaborated on a number of research projects over the last decade. Early in our association, we realized the naivete of each in the other's field. We deliberately set out to educate one another. In many respects this book is a stage in that process. We do not agree on everything that is said here, but, rather than water down the issues in compromise, we have chosen to air them so that the reader, who may equally disagree with the interpretation, will at least be aware of their existence.

Many of our colleagues in sociology and medicine have contributed to our thinking, and we have enjoyed debating the issues with most of them. Some we have referenced, and we have no doubt stolen the ideas of others without realizing their origins. It is a sin of omission for which we can only beg forgiveness and offer gratitude for the ideas.

Two very special people must be especially thanked. Nancy Robertson kept the coffee hot and interpreted our misunderstandings with wit and wisdom. Mary Ann Braunstein deciphered our scribbling and made it into readable typescript with skill and good humor. The fact that all four of us came out of the same Appalachian hills was not a disadvantage.

1
General systems theory

The system has gotten a bad name in recent years. Some people have wanted to "tear down the system," while others have wanted to "change the system." Still others have urged us to "work within the system." We suspect that many persons holding any one of these viewpoints would have difficulty in agreeing with each other as to what the system is, much less what it should be. The term used in these contexts refers to a variable set of political, social, and economic rules and practices that are a part of the inner workings of our society. To tear it down, change it, or work within it, requires at least some knowledge of what it is and how it works.

As far as we are aware, no one has complete knowledge as to how the system works. However, a set of concepts is being developed in order to help us view and understand better the various systems that are part of us and of which we are a part. Systems analysts believe that there are general concepts and principles which are common to many, if not all, systems. These concepts and principles make up general systems theory. By learning the concepts and principles, we gain an intellectual framework that can alert us to use our knowledge of the systems which we understand in order to gain knowledge of those systems we do not understand.

Elements of Systems

Rather than pursue an extensive exegesis and critique of what this or that theorist means by given system concepts, we prefer to present a brief outline with illustrations of how we shall use the concepts in this book. Any set of *elements* and their accompanying attributes that are related to one another in other than a totally random way may be considered a *system*. Such sets of elements, for example, might be subatomic particles, atoms, molecules, crystals, organelles, cells, organs, people, groups, or societies. From these examples it can be seen that the elements of one system may be systems in themselves. Atoms are made up of interacting particles; molecules are made up of interacting atoms; crystals and organelles are made up of interacting molecules, and so on (Miller, 1971).

However, a system is more than just the sum of its elements or subsystems (Hall and Fagen, 1956). An organic compound is not just the sum of the carbon and other atoms in the system but also depends on the position of these atoms relative to one another, the temperature of the system's environment, as well as other factors. The reaction of a family to the news that a daughter is illegitimately pregnant is not just the sum of the mother and father's attitudes toward illegitimacy but depends on such things as the prior relationship of the mother, father, and daughter; the prospect for the daughter's marriage; and the family's social position in the community.

When a given set of elements or systems combines to form a new system, it is called an *emergent* system. The positions of elements relative to one another in some definable space comprise the *organization* of the system. The movement of the elements relative to one another over time is the *process* of the system.

The space around physical elements is defined in three dimensions. With sufficiently precise and accurate measuring instruments, it is possible to locate a physical element at a definable point in space and time relative to other elements. If the elements can be precisely and accurately observed over time, the process of the movement of the elements relative to one another can be defined.

The power of science in studying any given system depends upon the precision and accuracy of the measuring instruments and the command of a comprehensible abstract system (model) to describe what the instruments are measuring. The abstractions invented by mathematicians have proved powerful instruments in describing the organization and process of nonliving systems and are now being used in the study of living systems. The geometry of the ancient Greeks and their successors provides us a tool for describing the location of elements in three-dimensional space at any given time. The calculus of Sir Isaac Newton allows us to describe the movement of any number of elements relative to one another over time and the forces involved in their movement. Mathematical statistics provide the tools to test whether or not these locations or movements are random.

Because neither we nor perhaps many of our readers are sufficiently well versed in mathematics, we shall not attempt to present mathematical models of the systems we shall discuss. In the case of many systems, such models are yet to be developed. The elements and their known or hypothesized relationships have to be described using less accurate and precise abstracting systems, namely language and oversimplified diagrams.

When an abstract system describes an empirical system precisely and accurately, the systems are said to be *isomorphic* (Coleman, 1964). Historically, mathematical systems sometimes were designed specifically to describe empirical systems. However, many mathematicians have created mathematical systems without any concern that the abstract elements of their mathematics represent the elements in any known empirical systems. Because of predictive power of isomorphic mathematical systems, scientists expend considerable effort trying to demonstrate isomorphism between a system of phenomena in which they are interested and an existing mathematical system.

Although these efforts have been partially successful, there are limitations on researching the "living" systems in which we are mainly interested here. Our values regarding life, particularly human life, restrict us from tampering with certain systems either for the purpose of precise and accurate measurement or experimentation (Katz, 1972). And, even if the data were always readily available, with today's specialization in science there are few scientists sufficiently knowledgeable in both the empirical systems and mathematical systems to discover all of the isomorphisms. Of course, mathematical systems which are isomorphic to some empirical systems may not exist.

Without pursuing the issue of when a system is living or not (Buckley, 1968), we should point out that living systems present behavior that is often thought to be different in kind from that of nonliving systems. Living systems often show such characteristics as extensive adaptation to changes (both external and internal), a degree of self-regulation, and purposive behavior. As a result, some theorists have resorted to explanations of the structure of a system based on its "purpose" or "function." A functionalist's explanation of family organization might include such statements as: "A woman's position as wife and mother in the home results from the necessity for society to replace its members through the bearing and rearing of children." Thus, the "effect," the family structure, is said to occur in time before the "cause," replacement of members. Such teleological explanations are untenable for a scientist (Rosenblueth, et al., 1943; Taylor, 1950; Rosenblueth and Weiner, 1950). Time is required for one element to act on another, and there is no scientifically verified instance in which time stood still, much less was reversed.

Input, Output, and Feedback

The invention of machines that are adaptive, self-regulating, and goal-seeking has forced theorists to question the assumption that these properties are unique to living systems (Buckley, 1967). Consider a thermostat and a heating unit as the elements in a system. The system adapts itself to the demands of the environment, is self-regulating, and pursues the purpose of maintaining a minimum temperature.

Elements from other systems in the environment that influence change in the elements of a given system are called *input* to that system. When the heat (input) in the environment of a thermostat-heater system reaches a preset minimum level, the thermostat activates the heater to produce heat. Heat from the heater is the *output* of the system, the element that leaves the system to become part of the environment. Thus, heat is both input to and output from the thermostat-heater system.

When the output of a system becomes or influences the input to the same system subsequently, the process is called *feed-*

4

back. The term feedback is something of a misnomer. The effects of the output on the system are not "back" in time. However, the term is in such widespread use that we shall not further confuse the issue by offering another here.

If the heater in our example has sufficient energy (another input) to raise the environmental heat above the minimum origally set by someone in the environment (another input), the thermostat will be modified and the heater will stop—until the environmental heat reaches the minimum level again (Figure 1–1). When an increase in output results in a decrease in subsequent input, or a decrease in output results in an increase in subsequent input, the relationship between output and input is said to be negative and the result is called *negative feedback*.

Thermostat-Heating System

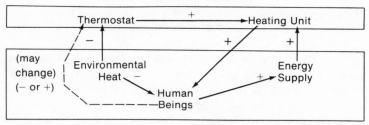

Environmental Systems

Figure 1-1. Diagram of Thermostat-Heating System and Relevant Systems in the Environment.

Of course, the feedback relationship may be more complex than that in the thermostat-heater system described. The output from system A may influence system B, which affects system C, which affects system D, which modifies the input to system A at a subsequent time. To establish whether feedback is positive or negative, one must assess whether or not the net relationship between output that has an effect on subsequent input to the system is negative or positive. Unfortunately, only a few biological and social systems have been studied with the precision and accuracy necessary to specify the nature of their feedback.

Positive feedback occurs when an increase in output results in a subsequent increase in input or when a decrease in output

5

brings about a future decrease in input. The consequences for systems with positive feedback and those with negative feedback are quite different. They have been characterized, respectively, as "deviation-amplifying" and "deviation-counteracting" (Maruyama, 1963).

A system with negative feedback tends to maintain itself within some limits determined by the system or its environment. The thermostat-heating system will maintain the temperature between a degree or so below the minimum set on the thermostat and a maximum set by the environment (weather or contiguous heating units). Adding a cooling unit to a system with the proper relationships causes the fluctuation in temperature to be narrowed to small deviations from a set average, depending, of course, on a sufficient energy supply and on the capacity (maximum energy conversion rate) of the heating and cooling units relative to the area in which the temperature is to be maintained. Thus, the system adapts to the environment and regulates itself in order to pursue a goal (in this case, maintenance of a specified temperature range).

Uninterrupted positive feedback in a system leads either to continued acceleration of change or to cessation of activity of that system. Accelerated change occurs when an increase in output contributes to a subsequent increase in input. A growth process is a good example. Consider the growth of a population. If two teenagers, male and female, were placed in an Eden-like environment and told to be fruitful and multiply, what would happen? Assume that they:

(1) accepted the charge, (2) taught it to subsequent generations, (3) begat an average of four offspring at an average of 20 years, (4) lived to an average age of 60 years and (5) developed no incest taboo.

The elements in the system (people), calculated from the birth of the first pair, would number approximately 28 after 60 years, 112 after 100 years, 3,444 after 200 years, and 117,262,000 after 500 years. The numbers of people in the system after 1,000 or more years become almost incomprehensible. Obviously such a system would, in time, have an effect on contiguous systems. (See Frederiksen, 1969 for an analysis of some complex feedback processes among population size and other systems).

A system may cease to operate when decreased output

results in a later decrease in input. The physician who discovers a nonserious heart murmur in a child but does not explain that the child's activity need not be curtailed may initiate such a process. The parents, operating under the assumption that heart patients should not participate in vigorous exercise, decrease the child's activities. As a result of sedentary living, the child may gain weight and use oxygen less efficiently, thereby increasing the amount of work his heart must do. The resulting shortness of breath and lethargy may reinforce the parents' perception that the child is ill, causing them to limit his activities even further. If this cycle continues without interruption on the part of an environmental element, such as new information from the physician or other source, the heart or some other essential subsystem could conceivably be affected to the point that essential processes cease. The system is then static; that is, the person dies prematurely.

System Boundaries, Levels, and Echelons

In the preceding illustration we have described the interaction of a number of elements, combinations of which could be considered as elements in a number of systems. Various physiological systems are involved in the child's weight, breathing, and heart activity. Mother, father, and child are elements in the family system. Adding the physician creates another system, which may be a patient-physician or a physician-family system depending on the elements involved. It may not always be easy to determine the elements that constitute a system, but there are usually clearcut boundaries through which inputs and outputs, respectively, must pass to enter and leave it. The *boundary* is the outer limit of a system, made up of elements and interactions of elements in the system that regulate input and output.

While the boundaries of some systems appear obvious (*e.g.,* a cell has a wall; the human body is covered by skin), they are not for others (*e.g.,* there is some controversy over the boundaries of some national territories, love, and the universe). Researchers interested in the organization or the interaction of a particular set of elements may have difficulty defining the boundaries of the systems of which the elements are a part.

Usually research questions are put in terms not of systems

but of causation, such as: What causes lung cancer? Numerous studies have shown that the probability of lung cancer is increased by ever greater increments of cigarette smoke and other air pollutants going into the lungs. Apparently this input, coupled with other factors, initiates the process called lung cancer in susceptible individuals. Therefore, it can be said, although inexactly, that smoking, in some cases, probably causes lung cancer. However, this tells us relatively little about the phenomenon called lung cancer and is not, in itself, helpful in identifying other causative agents.

The general systems theorist observes that cancer is a rapid growth process. Since such processes often result from positive feedback, it seems likely that output from some system is influencing subsequent increments in input to the system. But what is the unit from which the output is emerging and into which the input is going? One may view the cell as the unit of growth and look for inputs and outputs through cell walls. Or the chromosome may be the proper system with other elements of the cell considered as environment. If scientists knew the exact unit, they might be well on the way to solving the riddle of cancer. This example illustrates the type of thinking that forces an investigator to view phenomena in terms of the elements involved, the processes whereby they are changing, and the boundaries on these elements.

Related to the problem of defining boundaries of systems is the problem of specifying a system's level. The *level* of a system refers to its place in the submicroscopic to macroscopic hierarchy of systems. As noted earlier, a particular set of systems (*e.g.*, cells) can be elements of another system (*e.g.*, an organ). The input and output to and from a given system can only directly affect other systems at the same level and systems at the next higher and lower levels. The following example from a previous study in medical sociology will show why this is the case.

In the study one consistent finding is that people who show high achievement, such as high grades in school, have higher concentrations of uric acid in their blood or urine (a factor in a painful disease of the joints called gout) than do persons who show low achievement (Kasl, *et al.*, 1970). Achievement is a complex set of behaviors in a social system, such as a school. Uric acid is a compound, one of the outputs of the metabolic system's processing of certain proteins.

In order to have an effect on a behavioral system, a chemical system product such as uric acid would have to initiate a chain of events through a number of levels of systems. It may be an input to brain cells where it could alter molecular systems and the subsequent outputs to the nervous system. On the other hand, uric acid may have no effect, even indirect, on achievement behavior. Achievement behavior could indirectly affect uric acid production, but through what levels of systems? Eating behavior, sedentary living, or other factors could be involved but, again, indirectly through other systems. There could be some multilevel feedback between the two phenomena or they may only be spuriously correlated; that is, a third factor could affect them both so that they occur together frequently but have no effect, direct or indirect, on one another.

It is not necessary to investigate every link among the involved systems to rule out each possible explanation of the correlation. For example, the uric acid-brain-nervous system-achievement behavior chain could be ruled out by showing that uric acid does not breach the blood-brain barrier, a boundary around the nervous system that filters out a number of substances. To our knowledge no one has shown whether uric acid breaches the blood-brain barrier. If the investigator is aware of such particularly strong boundaries at particular levels, he should look there first.

The defining of elements, boundaries, and levels is not evident in the research of many behavioral scientists. For example, it is commonly found that males and females behave differently when presented with the same stimuli. Males are usually more aggressive than females; for example, they more often commit homicide and suicide than do females. The interpretation of the results may depend more on the theoretical orientation of the researcher than on the possible levels and boundaries of the systems involved. The sociologist often interprets sex differences to be the result of the social positions assigned to males and females and the roles (expected behaviors) of those positions. Although not mutually exclusive from the sociologist's interpretation, the psychologist is likely to place more emphasis on some learned mental state such as sexual identity. Usually, neither of these scientists is inclined to consider the behavioral biologist's likely interpretation that sex differences in aggression are genetically or hormonally based.

At least six levels of systems could be factors in sex differences in behavior:

1. the genetic system (XX, XY, or other rare combinations of chromosomes such as XYY); 2. gonadal systems (ovaries or testes and accompanying structures); 3. sex hormones (produced in various glands but primarily in the gonads); 4. external structures (genitalia, body build, distribution of body hair); 5. mental sets learned from parents and others (such as sexual identity); and 6. group assignment of social positions and roles (Mazur and Robertson, 1972).

The outputs of some of these systems act directly on contiguous systems and indirectly can affect most of the others. To attribute sex differences exclusively to one or the other of these systems is an oversimplification.

Aggressive behavior has been shown to be related to child-rearing practices (Sears, et al., 1958), frustrating situations (Dollard, et al., 1939; Berkowitz, 1969), aggression of other persons in the individual's environment (Bandura and Walters, 1963), impersonal aggressive stimuli in the environment (Berkowitz, 1968), obedience to authority (Milgram, 1963), a hormone called norepinephrine that is an output from the adrenal gland and from nerve endings (Funkenstein, et al., 1957), and to a hormone called testosterone that is an output from the adrenal gland in small concentrations in males and females and in larger concentrations from the testes in males (Persky, et al., 1971; Kreuz and Rose, 1972). It is clear that both social and hormonal factors are related to aggressive behavior. The systems of the brain apparently receive inputs from the social system and from other biological systems, and the brain's output, given particular combinations of inputs and internal processing, affects aggressive behavior. Unfortunately, our measures of elements of the brain are not yet sufficient for us to build an adequate model of its organization and processes. Therefore, it is not possible to say exactly what proportions of sex differences in aggression can be attributed to hormonal differences, differences in the social experiences of males and females, or other differences. It is often impossible or unfeasible to measure the elements of all relevant systems simultaneously in a given research project. However, when more than one system could be involved in the phenomenon in question, relevant elements of those systems should be measured if at all possible.

Levels refer to the horizontal organization of systems. Elements of larger systems such as hospitals, companies, and governments are usually organized vertically as well as horizontally. Such vertical divisions are called *echelons*. There may or may not be levels within a given echelon (Miller, 1971), although the greater the number of systems involved, the greater the likelihood that there are multiple levels. A small hospital might be organized into a medical department, a nursing department, and an administrative department. Each department is an echelon of the organization, and there may be a number of levels of groups in each echelon. If the hospital grows in size, each of these echelons may be divided. For example, the medical department might be organized into divisions of pediatrics, internal medicine, surgery, and obstetrics-gynecology.

It would be a tedious exercise for each research report to review all the possible systems involved in the phenomenon being studied and to define each element, boundary, level, and echelon therein. We shall not attempt to do so each time we take up a new topic in this book. In some cases this will be done to avoid tedium and in others because there may not be enough known about the systems involved to define precisely and accurately the elements, boundaries, and levels involved. Faced with the latter situation, one may arbitrarily define elements, boundaries, and levels until enough is learned about their interrelationships to develop a more accurate model.

By being aware of the possible variation in levels at which one is working, the boundaries involved (no matter how arbitrary), and the type of processes that are likely to lead to the results being observed, the reseacher is led through a sequence of redefining elements, making hypotheses regarding their relationships, and testing or re-observing them until the phenomena are understood. This point is especially relevant to physicians and sociologists. Physicians often are taught many facts that are stored for recall in particular instances but may have difficulty relating one set of facts to others. A physician may know that a given drug will relieve a certain symptom but be unable to relate the symptom to other observations about the patient, his family, or his social situation that may explain the occurrence of the symptom and suggest a different, more appropriate, therapy. Sociologists, on the other hand, talk a great deal about systems and the relationship between theory and research. In practice, however, a considerable amount of data gathering is done, sometimes without careful thought about the unit of analysis involved, the levels of the phenomena being related, and the positions of the phenomena in some larger unit. This is at least partially due to the fact that what passes for sociological theory is often too many levels of abstraction removed from the data, and contains misleading, if not untenable, propositions such as those found in the functionalist approach (Buckley, 1967).

The Black Box Notion

Even when it is impossible to measure the elements and their actions within the boundaries of a system, such as the brain, one may be able to measure enough inputs and outputs to make some inferences about their relationships. The thermostat-heating system with its two or three inputs and single output can be (and was) described without specifying the inner workings of the thermostat or the heater. The inner elements and processes of the system are said to be in a black box, unobservable or uninteresting for the time being.

Consideration of the number and nature of the inputs and outputs from a system treated as a black box illustrates the oversimplification of many of our inferences about systems such as the brain. Berrien (1968) points out that a relatively simple system with eight two-state ("on" and "off") inputs and two two-state outputs has 2,256 possible connections of input and output states. The brain has many more than eight input and two output nerve channels, not to mention hormonal and other biochemical inputs and outputs through the bloodstream. It may be useful to speak of personality as comprised of such elements as id, ego, and superego, as Freud did, or of multidimensions of personality derived from peoples' answers to questionnaires, as many psychologists do, as long as we realize that these are grossly oversimplified theoretical constructs.

Mind and Matter

There is a long-standing philosophical controversy over whether or not mind and brain are separate entities. This contro-

12

versy is likely to continue as long as the organization and processes of the elements of the brain are not understood. Enough is known, however, to conclude that the known elements of the brain are sufficiently complex to encode, store, and decode the amounts of information that occur in inputs and outputs. The nucleic acids are likely candidates for the storage of information in the brain (Bogoch, 1968). The DNA (deoxyribonucleic acid) molecule is the basic element in information storage and transmission in heredity. Its biochemical cousin, RNA (ribonucleic acid), has similar information encoding, storage, and decoding properties (Beadle and Beadle, 1966) and is more than plentiful enough in each individual's approximately 10 billion cells in the cortex of the human brain to handle the amounts of information involved.

Miller (1971) notes that information exists in "observable bundles, units, or changes of matter-energy" called *markers*. Is thought something other than organization and processes among markers? If there is no distinction between thought and energy-matter, then to speak of the "physical" sciences (physics, chemistry, biology and the like) as though other sciences (*e.g.*, psychology and sociology) were not physical sciences may be a false distinction. The abstractions generated by the brains of people, whether mathematical systems, language systems, or social positions in human groups, all probably have a physical reality, at least in the molecular structure of the brains of the people in which they are stored or generated. If they become output from these people, they are physically available as input to others, as sound waves, written symbols, or whatever.

These outputs from a given individual, to the degree that they are inputs to other individuals, become a part of social reality. The human infant, as well as the offspring of many other living creatures, is not sufficiently developed for some time after birth to seek and use the matter and energy necessary to sustain it as a living system. Other sufficiently developed creatures must provide these inputs. As the infant receives food and warmth, it also receives the energy waves we call sound and may respond with sounds or other outputs. Thus begins the process of *interaction*, the exchange of inputs and outputs between individuals, the process whereby the social reality is transmitted, or sometimes modified, from one generation to the next. Socially, one person's input is another person's output.

Social Systems

As with the evolution of biological systems, the historical emergence of social interaction patterns cannot be completely traced. Whether the process of development of individual interaction skills recapitulates the evolution of the process is not known. Comparisons of human beings and other primates (apes, monkeys, prosimians) suggest interesting parallels between the emergence of biological structures and certain aspects of social interaction such as mating, juvenile play, and social ranking (Mazur and Robertson, 1972). Here we need only define the elements of social systems and discuss some of the principles necessary to understand our later treatment of these systems.

Among the basic elements in human social systems are people and groups. Two or more people interacting nonrandomly make up a *group*. Interaction is nonrandom to the degree that the brains of the persons interacting have received prior inputs from similar environments. When the input is perception of a few gestures or sounds, such as smiles and crying (Darwin, 1965), the neural processing and resultant outputs may be a species characteristic and thus similar for almost all human beings. However, most of the sounds and gestures used in interaction in a given group are arbitrary. If people interacting do not have a substantial number of similar markers obtained from prior interaction in prior environments, their interaction is likely to be almost totally random and short-lived. A person asking directions in a country whose language he doesn't understand is a good example.

Persons in interaction over time tend to modify their commonly shared markers and create new ones. A particular sound pattern, gesture or written notation may have a unique referent in a particular group. Since persons are usually elements in more than one group, these markers are transferred from one group to another in their brains or in other matter-energy systems such as books, punched cards, television, and radio. In time, these markers may come to be shared by large numbers of people.

We refer to commonly shared markers as *language*. Children receive and store the language of the persons who take care of them, usually but not necessarily their biological parents, during the first few years of life. Language may change somewhat as the

14

caretaker and child interact. The child may receive and store a wider variety of languages as he interacts in other groups, and he receives as inputs the markers of other groups stored in written language or other media.

As persons act and interact in groups, the various inputs alter markers in their brains so that who is acting, the actions, and the environmental circumstances of the actions are organized and stored. When an interaction is repeated in a similar fashion under similar circumstances, another set of markers, representing anticipation or expectation of action under the similar circumstances, develops. As the child interacts with his caretakers, expectations of certain actions are often conveyed to him such as when to eat. In turn, the child may make his expectations known, *e.g.*, by crying when he is hungry.

Expectations of behavior that are shared by persons in a group are called *norms*. They are the rules of behavior. Just as with language, norms tend to be carried from one group to another and are often shared in widely different groups. As in biological and inanimate systems, the elements of social systems are altered relative to their contiguity in time and space. The greater the separation of groups by space, time, or frequency of overlap in membership, the greater is the likelihood that their languages, norms, and other elements will be different.

Formal and Informal Norms

Usually among the shared norms are those that define the boundary of the system, regulating input and output. These norms, general to all group members, say who can be a member, how one becomes a member, and how one loses membership. Other norms apply only to certain positions within a group. When the positions in a group and the cluster of norms defining expected behaviors of persons who occupy those positions have been recorded in markers external to the brains of the group members, we say that the organization of the group is *formal*. Constitutions, laws, charters, and organization charts are examples of markers that define the formal organization of various groups. In some groups, general norms as well as the positions and position-related norms exist only as markers in the brains of the people involved. We then say that the group's organization is *informal*.

15

Sociologists refer to a given position in a group as *status* and the cluster of norms defining expected behaviors of that position as the *role* of that status. The latter term obviously was borrowed from dramatics. "All the world's a stage, and all the men and women merely players: they have their exits and their entrances; and one man in his time plays many parts." (Wm. Shakespeare, *As You Like It,* Act II, Scene 7, Line 139.)

People and the statuses they occupy in most formally organized groups are distinguishable. The status of chief surgeon in a hospital is occupied by many persons over time. However, frequently in informal and occasionally in formal groups, some or all of the members may think the person and the status that person occupies synonymous. In the society of the United States, as well as many others, the laws define a father as the male biological parent and a mother as the female biological parent of a given child. Even though one or both of these persons may be no longer in the group caring for the child or have been replaced by other persons, they are still considered the "real" parents of the child. Therefore, it is useful analytically to distinguish the statuses in a group from the persons occupying those statuses.

The formal statuses, roles, and general norms of formally organized groups may change periodically. Constitutions are amended, charters are rewritten, organizational tables are changed. However, the people in the groups are in frequent interaction. This interaction tends to create an informal organization that may be more important in understanding the behavior of group members than the formal organization. Anyone who looks at an organization chart or procedure manual of a group and assumes that it conveys the total organization and process of the group is naive.

General Systems Principles

The basic question posed by the general systems theorist is whether or not the organization and processes of social systems, psychological systems, biological systems, and inanimate systems can be understood using the same principles. Our scope is much narrower but, since all of these systems are involved in the material to be covered, the general systems approach is appropriate.

In this chapter we have attempted to outline some contemporary thoughts about general systems theory and to cast in the

16

general systems mold some of the sociological concepts that we shall use to examine health and medical care systems. We have stated a few principles of the organization and processes of systems which may be applicable to all systems. To state and explain all of the principles that have been proposed by general systems theorists would require more space than is available. We shall introduce some of these principles at appropriate points when discussing particular systems.

Before proceeding, we must provide a cautionary note. General systems principles are based on analogy, a statement that system A is like system B, C, or D. Analogies are powerful tools in generating hypotheses about how a system works by suggesting to us that one system, at least superficially, is behaving like another system we understand. Because one system resembles another system does not mean that the resemblance is complete.

A rapid increase in the number of elements in a system may result from positive feedback, but it is not necessarily so. Rapid growth can also occur because the ratio of matter-energy input to matter-energy output is increasing, possibly because of an alteration in boundary elements. The regulation of temperature in a human body and a room equipped with a thermostat-heating-cooling system may be similar in some respects (both undoubtedly involve negative feedback) but not others (the temperature-sensing mechanisms are undoubtedly different).

The point is that each system must be observed empirically to establish that it follows a given principle. Statements of analogies are not sufficient as conclusive evidence. If general systems theory provides a language for the unification of the sciences and hypotheses, by analogy, that lead to new discoveries, it will have more than served its purpose. If general principles are empirically verified as applicable to all systems, the seemingly unmanageable complexity of ourselves and our environment may become more manageable.

2
Social systems
and disease

Gertrude Stein said, "A rose is a rose is a rose." Perhaps so, but different persons, looking at the flower, are likely to see different things. The botanist's vision is unlikely to be the same as the poet's. We each see the rose, but our training and experience have given us different intellectual frameworks and it is within these frameworks that we perceive reality.

Consider bubonic plague, or Black Death, as it was called in the Middle Ages. It was attributed at various times and places to demons and evil spirits, or to the wrath of God, or to the vengeance of an oppressed minority until the discovery of the plague bacillus in 1894 (Hirst, 1953). The ancient Egyptians and Babylonians respectively, held to the evil spirit and demon theories. The writer of 1 Samuel 5 thought that widespread deaths among the Philistines, associated with "emerods in their secret parts," was wrought by the God of Israel because the Philistines had placed the Ark of God in the house of Dagon, the Philistine God. "A swelling in the region of the groin (emerods), due to an inflammatory enlargement of a group of lymphatic glands, is the most characteristic sign of plague" (Hirst, 1953). Ironically, in 1348 over most of Europe, there were rumors that the plague was the result of poison placed in the water wells by Jews. Thousands of Jews were killed by their gentile neighbors.

Although theories of the causes and treatment of human maladies have been changed radically by scientific philosophy and discovery, vast areas of unexplored and unknown terrain in the human condition and its maladies remain. The attribution of mankind's problems to demons, devils, Jews, and even God continues in some circles. The alternative explanations discovered or proposed by scientists are not always accepted by other scientists, much less by the general public.

The Epidemiological Model

Epidemiologists are specialists who study the systems involved in the distributions of diseases. Some sociologists have become involved in epidemiological research. Traditionally, epidemiologists have viewed the human organism as the host of invading, damage-producing agents. Once an agent, such as the plague bacillus, is associated with the damage, the epidemiologist asks such questions as: Where is the agent found in the environment and what characteristics of the environment increase or decrease its presence? How does the agent reach human beings and in what quantities? What is the portal of entry into human organisms? How long is the agent in people before damage ensues, and, indeed, are all these whom it enters damaged? Is the agent communicable from person to person, and if so, how and during what period of the disease cycle? What characteristics of the host (*e.g.,* nutrition, stress, genetic factors, immunity) make him more or less susceptible to the disease (Fox, *et al.,* 1970)?

Sometimes, because of poor theories, poor research design, or poor measurement techniques, false answers will be obtained before the valid model of the damage-producing process is discovered. After the identification of the plague bacillus in diseased humans, some investigators thought it was also present in some vermin, such as rats (correct) and cockroaches (incorrect), and in domestic animals, such as pigs and poultry (incorrect), and that it entered people in contaminated food (incorrect). Others thought the bacillus was transmitted directly from person to person, but identification and isolation of those with plague failed to stop the

20

spread of the disease. Despite the fact that plague bacillus had been shown not to survive long outside a body, mass disinfection campaigns were attempted. "In some instances, there was evidence that the flooding of drains with quantities of disinfectants drove infected rats into nearby houses and led to the subsequent death of the inhabitants" (Hirst, 1953).

In a series of observations and experiments, P. L. Simond showed that plague resulted when the bacillus was introduced into a break of the skin but not when placed on its intact surface. Noting that the typical lesions of plague were found more often in the thin skin near the ankle than near abrasions on the sole of the foot, he suspected that a blood-sucking insect carried the bacillus rather than its being picked up from floor and other surfaces. He subsequently demonstrated the bacilli were in fleas found on infected rats but not in fleas on healthy rats. After a number of experiments by Simond and others, it was shown that fleas did transmit the disease from infected to healthy rats. However, the results were not immediately accepted because the findings in these experiments were not always consistent, presumably because the wrong species of flea, immune rats, or some unknown factor was involved in the experiments. Eventually, with the removal of rats or fleas from human dwellings and the development of vaccines and of medical treatment, the incidence and severity of bubonic plague was essentially eradicated (Hirst, 1953).

The successful use of the agent-host-environment model in the discovery of the ecology of numerous diseases recommends its continued use in investigating modern killers of man. The leading "causes" of death in the industrialized areas of the world are heart and circulatory diseases, cancer, and injury in "accidents." The terms "causes" and "accidents" are placed in quotes to indicate that these concepts require explication; in their common usage, these terms have connotations that are misleading. The term "accident" often has the connotation of an unexpected, uncontrollable event, yet these events are not more unexpected than the onset of some diseases and there are known methods to control the frequency and severity of many of them (Haddon, 1968). Again, as with the control of plague, our conceptual framework, if incorrect, can lead our investigations and therapeutic endeavors in false or even counterproductive directions.

21

Social Correlates of Disease

Social factors may be involved in the frequency and severity of disease and injury in at least three ways. First, social conditions may affect the exposure of the organism to noxious agents in the environment. Second, the internal states of the organism, which, in themselves, may produce disease or contribute to resistance to disease, may be altered through interaction with the social environment. Finally, the social system may affect medical care in such a way that the control of disease is increased or decreased. Substantial proportions of subsequent chapters of this book are devoted to social factors in medical care. Here we shall present a few examples of current thinking regarding social factors in exposure to noxious agents and in altering elements internal to the organism.

Although societies as a whole tend to share a common culture, all persons do not have equal access to all elements of it. People with similar income, jobs, and education tend to interact with one another more than they do with people different from themselves relative to these factors. Those who have inherited wealth, or who have better paying jobs, or more education tend to acquire the more desirable artifacts and land. Clusters of people, groups, and living areas tend to be differentiated into layers, called social classes. In societies where these layers are formalized, they are called castes and the layers are clearly distinguishable. In societies where the layers are not formalized, the class lines are not as easily distinguishable but there is, nevertheless, considerable distance from upper to lower socioeconomic classes. Cultural differences between the higher and lower classes within one society ordinarily are not as large as those between societies, but the differences in language, norms, and artifacts are such that interaction among persons from different social classes is often difficult.

One of the more dramatic examples of these factors in exposure to injury occurred when the supposedly unsinkable ship, the "Titanic," struck an iceberg and sank in 1912. Social-class differences among passengers were reflected in first-, second-, and third-class accommodations. "The official casualty list showed that only four first class female passengers (three voluntarily chose to stay on the ship) of a total of 143 were lost. Among second-class passengers, 15 of 93 females drowned; and among the third class, 81 of

179 female passengers went down with the ship" (Lord, 1955). Usually social class is less formalized than that reflected in travel accommodations, but one need only examine who lives downwind from polluting smokestacks in almost any city to understand the differential exposure to noxious agents in different social classes. Only recently, when pollution began to affect everyone, regardless of social position, has it received widespread attention. The brown haze over our cities and the multicolored slime in our rivers and lakes are evident to almost everyone. We are only beginning to realize the consequences to health of these various forms of pollution (and the many unseen forms as well).

One example of pollution, air pollution by automobiles, illustrates how social processes involving positive feedback systems can lead to lethal contaminants in the environment. Through an intricate political process, in 1956 the U.S. Congress passed and President Dwight D. Eisenhower signed the Federal Highway Act, paving the way for the establishment of the Highway Trust Fund. All existing federal taxes on motor fuel; tire or tube rubber; and new truck, bus, and trailer sales were henceforth earmarked for the fund. Increases in these and other taxes on heavy vehicle use, retread rubber, and lubricating oil were added in subsequent years, further increasing the vast sums of money raised. These funds could only be used for Interstate Highway construction and federal aid road improvement. The fund was originally intended to expire in 1972, but the Federal Aid Highway Act of 1970 extended it through 1977 (Kelley, 1971).

To those who enjoy riding on the Interstate Highway system, this may seem to be a good thing. However, this funding system initiated a positive feedback chain of more highways–more cars–more taxes–more highways. Actually the chain is more elaborate (Figure 2–1). The availability of multilaned highways from the center of the city to the surrounding countryside contributed to an accelerated movement of people farther out of the city, commuting to work in the city in their automobiles. Many families purchased second or more cars. Driving farther, they produced more taxes to build more roads. The increased glut of traffic and the accompanying noise and pollution in the cities provoked more people to move farther out. Those profiting from the system exerted political pressure to keep it going. Only recently has a counter-lobby developed

23

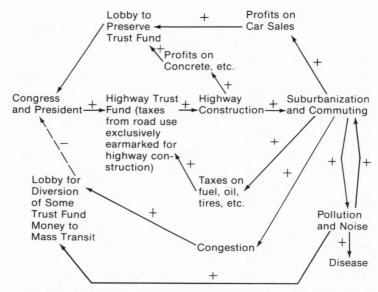

Figure 2-1. The Highway Trust Fund and Its Consequences as a Positive Feedback System.

to try to divert some of the funds to mass transit or other uses. The broken line in Figure 2–1 indicates that this counter-lobby has not yet been effective in converting the system to a negative feedback, and, therefore, more stable, system. Attempts to control pollutants emitted from vehicles by modifying the engines and exhaust systems are underway, but their success in substantially reversing the concentrations in the environment is problematic at this point.

The total consequences of the noxious agents in pollution from motor vehicles in terms of disease may never be known. A panel of scientists told a U.S. Senate committee in 1974 that they estimated 4,000 deaths and four million person days of restricted activity per year caused by polluting automobile exhaust emissions in urban areas (National Academy of Sciences, 1974).

Intake of lead or carbon monoxide in sufficient concentrations can be fatal. Concentrations in the atmosphere alone have not yet approached fatal levels in otherwise healthy persons not exposed

24

Social systems and disease

to these noxious agents from other sources. However, based on medical examiner records in one city, it has been estimated that over 500 persons in the United States die each year in vehicles where carbon monoxide has leaked into the passenger compartment (Baker, *et al.,* 1972). An unknown number of children die each year from lead poisoning, most of which is ingested in paint and plaster chips in deteriorating buildings (see the bibliography in Campbell and Mergard, 1972). Lead from automobile exhausts, either in the atmosphere or settled on objects which children placed in their mouths, contributes to the problem. Of course, the deterioration of the buildings in the inner cities is to some degree a result of the suburbanization process, which was partially a function of the highway-automobile syndrome described above.

Nonfatal concentrations of lead and carbon monoxide can do serious damage to nervous and other systems. Mental performance begins to deteriorate at carboxyhemoglobin (carbon monoxide in the hemoglobin) concentrations of 5 percent or more, concentrations commonly reached in persons who smoke a pack of cigarettes a day (DuBois, *et al.,* 1968). Persons who smoke heavily and also breathe the air on congested streets and highways reach higher concentrations. The carbon monoxide from cigarettes, automobile exhausts, and other sources attaches itself to hemoglobin and prevents the normal transportation of oxygen.

In persons with heart disease the consequences have been shown to be particularly serious, even in nonsmokers. Aronow, *et al.* (1972) studied the effects of a 90-minute drive in rush-hour freeway traffic on cardiac functioning in heart patients. During one trip the patients breathed normally, and during a second trip they breathed compressed purified air. Carboxyhemoglobin averaged 5 percent after breathing freeway air but less than 1 percent after breathing the purified air. The amount of exercise the patients could do before the onset of angina (chest pain) was significantly less after breathing freeway air than after breathing purified air. Other measures of heart functioning also showed significant deterioration after breathing freeway air as compared to the purified air.

To this litany of ill consequences of pollution we must add the energy crisis and all of its secondary effects and injury in and by motor vehicles. Shortages of petroleum used in making fertilizer threaten the food supply. The costs of plastics, drugs, and other

25

products, manufactured from petroleum and used in medical care, have greatly increased. Although the fatality rate per miles driven on Interstate Highways is lower than on other roads (and decreasing even more with the almost nationwide imposition of 55 m.p.h. speed limits), the total of deaths as a result of increased travel is undoubtedly higher than would have occurred without such a road system. In the 1970's motor vehicle related fatalities were averaging over 1,000 per week and injuries involving restricted activity for a day or more were averaging 13,000 per day (National Health Survey, 1972).

With this illustration as a starting point, the reader is invited to investigate the social processes that have led to other environmental hazards. What are the social processes that contribute to the production and use of products that contain such biologically damaging materials as mercury (Hartung and Dinman, 1972)? What are the social processes that contribute to the disposal of these products or materials so that they end up in air, water, or the food chain system?

Social Factors and Internal Organismic States

Social factors not only contribute to the probability that the organism will be exposed to noxious agents, they may also affect the state of the organism in terms of resistance to disease. Internal physiological status of the organism may be altered by interaction with the social and physical environment so that disease occurs without noxious physical agents actually entering from the environment. Central to this notion is the concept of stress.

Hans Selye (1950) in the 1920's and 1930's described what he called the general adaptation syndrome. He found in a series of brilliant experiments that almost any stress, such as heat, cold, injury, infection, or simply taping an animal to a table surface, resulted in the excretion of the adrenal gland (located over the kidneys) hormones into the bloodstream. It was later learned that the pituitary gland (at the base of the brain) controlled the release of the hormones from the adrenal cortex, through the release of adrenocorticotrophic hormone (ACTH). It was found that the ACTH from the pituitary and output from the adrenal glands were monitored in the brain and that their release was determined by a substance released from the brain that affected the pituitary. Thus, in addition to the nervous system, there was discovered a biochemical feedback system in the body, operating primarily through the bloodstream. A deficiency or overabundance of these hormones may produce or exacerbate a wide variety of diseases (Selye, 1950, 1962, 1964, 1968). Stressors, by increasing or decreasing various hormones to maladaptive levels, may increase the probability of incidence or severity of the diseases.

There are a number of definitions of stress (Levine and Scotch, 1970). Some researchers have used stress to refer to the environmental stimuli that activate the general adaptation syndrome, while others use the term to refer to psychological reactions to the external stimuli. Since the entire spectrum of events that can lead to hormonal arousal is not yet known, it seems reasonable to refer to the external stimuli as stressors and to say that the organism is stressed to the degree that hormonal or other systems are aroused. Perhaps with better understanding of the ways in which the brain processes the external stimuli, a precise definition of stress will be possible.

Social, biological, and medical scientists have found that various social conditions thought to be stressful are correlated with the incidence or severity of various diseases, including those that involve external physical, biological, and chemical agents. In the two-week period preceding the onset of streptococcal throat infections in children, events such as death of grandparents, change of residence, father's loss of job, and unusual pressures on the children have been shown to occur four times as often as in the two-week period afterward (Meyer and Haggerty, 1962). The streptococcus does the damage, but the social stressors apparently alter body states in such a way as to increase susceptibility.

In a large-scale survey of an area of Manhattan (Srole, *et al.,* 1962), respondents were classified as to degree of impairment of mental functioning. Impairment was found to be higher in proportion to number of potential stressors: parents' poor mental health, parents' poor physical health, childhood broken home, parents' character negatively perceived, parental quarrels, disagreements with parents, respondents' poor physical health, work worries, socioeconomic worries, poor interpersonal affiliation, marital worries, and parental worries (Langner and Michael, 1963). Since the incidence or reporting of a number of these factors could be influenced by the disease, the possible causal role of these factors remains in doubt. Lower socioeconomic status also was correlated with increased impairment, independent of the other factors.

Numerous studies have found the so-called mental diseases as well as other diseases to be more frequent in lower socioeconomic groups (Lerner, 1969; Fried, 1969). These studies are valuable in pointing to possible factors in the etiology of the diseases, but more refined studies must be done to filter out the particular factors involved in lower socioeconomic status that may contribute to the diseases. In some cases the causal sequence may be the opposite: disease may contribute to a downward drift in socioeconomic status. In other cases, an element of lower socioeconomic status, such as occupation, may increase the likelihood of exposure to noxious environmental agents (Hunter, 1969). Or, low socioeconomic status itself may be sufficiently stressful to increase the likelihood of some diseases.

Many of the questions raised by these studies may be answered by more refined measures of the degree to which particular events are stressful and by better research designs using these measures. What appears to be a major step in the direction of better measurement is the development of the Social Readjustment Rating Scale (Holmes and Rahe, 1967; Masuda and Holmes, 1967). To estimate the relative readjustment required after certain events, respondents in a survey were asked to rate the amount of readjustment to these events relative to an arbitrary score of 500 assigned to the readjustment required after marriage. The instructions to the respondents were equivalent to saying: If marriage requires 500 units of readjustment, how many units would death of a spouse require? The life events presented to the respondents and the average (mean) value (divided by ten) assigned to them by the respondents are presented in Figure 2–2. Note, for example, that death of a spouse, average score 100, was estimated as requiring about twice as much readjustment as marriage.

Comparing a number of groups, the researchers found remarkable agreement among average scores of the relative magnitude of perceived readjustment required by these events. A number of retrospective and a few prospective studies have been done relating the Social Readjustment Rating Scale to illness onset (Holmes and Masuda, 1970). These studies generally support the hypothesis

28

Figure 2-2. Social Readjustment Rating Scale*

Rank	Life Event	Mean Value
1	Death of spouse	100
2	Divorce	73
3	Marital separation	65
4	Jail term	63
5	Death of close family member	63
6	Personal injury or illness	53
7	Marriage	50
8	Fired at work	47
9	Marital reconciliation	45
10	Retirement	45
11	Change in health of family member	44
12	Pregnancy	40
13	Sex difficulties	39
14	Gain of new family member	39
15	Business readjustment	39
16	Change in financial state	38
17	Death of close friend	37
18	Change to different line of work	36
19	Change in number of arguments with spouse	35
20	Mortgage over $10,000	31
21	Foreclosure of mortgage or loan	30
22	Change in responsibilities at work	29
23	Son or daughter leaving home	29
24	Trouble with in-laws	29
25	Outstanding personal achievement	28
26	Wife begin or stop work	26
27	Begin or end school	26
28	Change in living conditions	25
29	Revision of personal habits	24
30	Trouble with boss	23
31	Change in work hours or conditions	20
32	Change in residence	20
33	Change in schools	20
34	Change in recreation	19
35	Change in church activities	19
36	Change in social activities	18
37	Mortgage or loan less than $10,000	17
38	Change in sleeping habits	16
39	Change in number of family get-togethers	15
40	Change in eating habits	15
41	Vacation	13
42	Christmas	12
43	Minor violations of the law	11

*Holmes and Rahe, 1967.

that higher scores on the scale are significantly associated with both the incidence and severity of some types of illness. In one of these studies, 232 patients with 42 diseases completed the Schedule of Recent Social Experience, giving the time of incidence of any of the readjustment events that occurred in their lives during the two years preceding their illness (Wyler, *et al.*, 1971). In the case of some diseases such as arthritis, the Rating Scale of Seriousness of Illness, developed on the basis of physician agreement, was strongly correlated with the amount of readjustment required for the recorded experiences.

While a vast improvement in measurement, the Social Readjustment Scale does not completely resolve the problem of predicting disease from stressful events. If we can equate "readjustment" and "stress," it suggests that certain events are about equally stressful among a wide variety of groups of people and that one can use the relative magnitude of the stressfulness of these events to predict probable onset and severity of certain diseases. However, it does not include all of the possible life events that may produce significant stress. This is not intended as criticism of the scale but simply points out that the sources of stress are legion. If a scale could be developed to account for all the factors that produce the greater magnitudes of stress, the list of items would be very long indeed.

As an illustration of another set of the many possible social stresses, consider the hypothesis of Dodge and Martin (1970) that the frequency of certain diseases in a society is correlated with low status integration. Status integration refers to the compatibility of the social positions which a person occupies in society. For example, because of limitations on her time and energy, a female lawyer with children may find it difficult to be both a mother and a lawyer. The expectations of her husband, parents, children, and the law firm are likely to be to some degree incompatible (role conflict). According to Dodge and Martin (1970), the following chain of events is likely to result from incompatible statuses and role conflicts: incompatible status⟶role conflict⟶nonconformity⟶instability in social relationships⟶stress⟶disease.

Using census data on the distributions of populations by such factors as age, sex, race, and marital status, Dodge and Martin (1970) constructed indices of status integration based on the relative frequency of numbers of people in certain combinations of these status groupings. Using death rates from certain diseases in the populations, the indices of status integration and mortality rates were shown to be inversely correlated in most cases.

The results are suggestive but are not an adequate test of the hypothesis. The persons who died may not have been the persons in the incompatible statuses. As mentioned earlier, certain statuses are more likely to directly expose persons to noxious agents than others. Furthermore, the fact that few people are found in certain combinations of statuses and many are found in others is not necessarily indicative of the relative incompatibility of particular combinations of statuses. Also certain combinations of particular types of status have been shown to be more stressful than others (Jackson, 1962; Jackson and Burke, 1965). When a person is assigned a status because of his own accomplishments, we say that the status is achieved. However, some statuses are assigned on the basis of characteristics such as race or sex over which the individual has no control. These are called ascribed statuses. Persons with high ascribed but low achieved status (such as a white person with low education) reported significantly more stress symptoms in a national survey than did persons with congruent statuses or high achieved but low ascribed status (such as a black person with high education).

An inadequate test of a hypothesis does not disprove the hypothesis. Some types of incompatible statuses do lead to increased stress and perhaps to a greater probability of disease. Whether the process is a one-way effect of sociological on biological systems through the levels of phenomena hypothesized by Martin and Dodge remains to be demonstrated.

The theories discussed thus far only consider the possibility that social phenomena produce stress and stress produces adverse biological consequences in the organism. The abnormal hormone concentrations that Selye and others have shown to be a factor in a number of diseases could be simply a consequence of long-term stress resulting from some of the social factors discussed. However, the sustained high or low hormone concentrations could also be a result of positive feedback systems, perhaps precipitated but not necessarily maintained by the social factors noted. To consider this possibility, we must briefly review some of the neurohormonal systems and some basic studies in social psychology.

31

Interaction of Biological and Social Systems

In spite of accumulating evidence to the contrary (Mazur and Robertson, 1972), sociologists have resisted the notion that biological factors affect social behavior to any significant degree. This sort of bias can blind the researcher to significant research problems or explanations for his data. If one thinks that social systems can have effects on biological systems, through exposure to noxious agents, poor nutrition, stress, and the like, but that biological systems cannot have effects on social systems, then he has ruled out the possibility of biosocial feedback, which could be involved in a number of diseases.

To illustrate the possibility of biosocial feedback in the process of the development of disease, let us first briefly look at some of the known neurohormonal systems. Figure 2–3 shows the flow of hormones from the pituitary gland to various target glands and organs. Although the overall pattern of hormonal balance is yet to be described (Mason, 1968), it is known that the brain acts as a monitor, something like a thermostat, and regulates the hormonal systems.

The feedback systems involved in the regulation of hormones known to be particularly susceptible to reaction to stressors are illustrated in Figure 2–4. On the left is the adrenal-cortical system. The brain monitors the amount of hormones from the adrenal cortex needed to maintain certain types of metabolism. When additional amounts of the hormones are required, corticotrophin releasing factor goes from the brain through the blood stream to the pituitary gland, there stimulating the release of adrenocorticotrophic hormone (ACTH). ACTH flows through the blood to the adrenal cortex and stimulates the release of the various steroids that are used in metabolism. Note that, when operating normally, this is a negative feedback system. Too little of the steroid hormones initiates the chain of events to increase their subsequent production, and an excess at a given time will result in a subsequent lack of production. Physicians who use adrenocortical steroids, such as cortisone, for therapeutic purposes must be careful not to damage the system permanently. Too much cortisone administered artificially for too long a time can result in atrophy of the adrenal cortex to the point that it is irreparable.

32

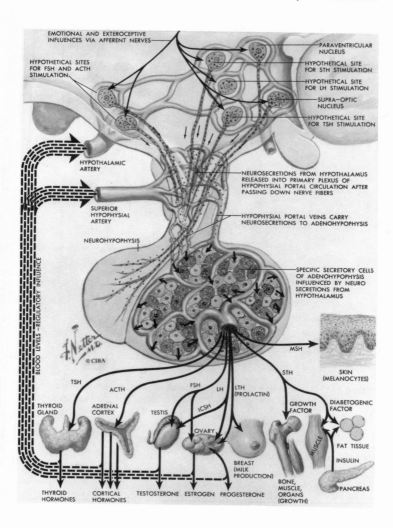

Figure 2-3. Circulatory flow between the hypothalamus, and anterior pituitary gland, and other organs. (Copyright 1965 CIBA Pharmaceutical Company, Division of CIBA Corporation, reproduced with permission from THE CIBA COLLECTION OF MEDICAL ILLUSTRATIONS by Frank H. Netter, M.D.)

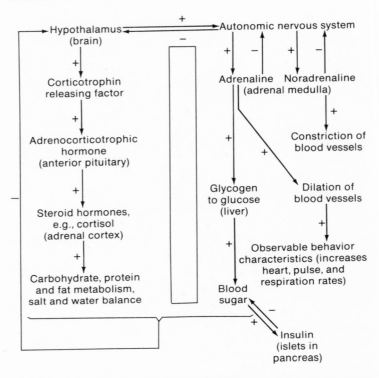

Figure 2-4. Greatly oversimplified schema of some relationships among nervous systems, hormone systems, and metabolic system.

When the organism is stressed, there is a time lag before the elevation of hormones from the adrenal cortex. However, the hormones of the adrenal medulla, shown to the right of the solid line in Figure 2–4, are more directly connected to the nervous system and may be elevated seconds after the organism perceives a stressful event. Adrenaline is important in the metabolism of sugar, and both adrenaline and noradrenaline affect blood flow and the associated heart, pulse, and respiration rates. The latter are observable behavioral characteristics that are important in our subsequent discussion of possible biosocial feedback.

Based on the known association of adrenaline-like responses with some forms of mental illness and the association of adrenaline with fright and of noradrenaline with aggressive behavior in animals, Funkenstein and his associates (1957) designed a study to investigate the correlation of personality and social background characteristics with indicators of hormonal reaction to stressful situations. One situation involved the participant's trying to tell a story while hearing his own voice delayed slightly through earphones. The inevitable result, stammering, was accompanied by a mild electrical shock. In the second situation, participants were given arithmetic problems to solve without pencil and paper. Incorrect answers were greeted by caustic comments regarding the participants' abilities. Each participant's physical reactions in these situations were classified as adrenaline-like or noradrenaline-like. When asked how they felt in the situations, some participants tended to be angry at the experimenters (anger-out), some tended to be angry with themselves (anger-in), and others tended to express anxiety. Comparing the verbal and physiological responses, the researchers found that anger-out responses were associated with noradrenaline-like responses and that anger-in and anxiety were associated with adrenaline-like responses.

The stress reactions, upon first encounter with the stress situation, were also correlated with the participants' recall of their relationships with their parents. The anger-out group more frequently characterized their mothers as warm and affectionate while their fathers were seen as stern and distant. Those who described their father as mild and affectionate while their mother was the primary source of affection were more often in the anger-in group. Anxious responses occurred more often in those whose mother was seen as both authority and source of affection, their father being either absent or dominated by the mother.

However, the recall of relationships with parents was not correlated with the pattern of response over three encounters with the stressful situation. The overall pattern in three situations was classified as follows:

(1) mastery—no severe anxiety in the first two encounters and performance anxiety or no emotion in the third encounter; (2) delayed mastery—severe anxiety in the first or second encounter and no emotion or performance anxiety in the third encounter; (3) unchanged reaction—the same reaction, excluding severe anxiety, in all three encounters;

(4) deteriorated reaction—severe anxiety in the third encounter regardless of the responses in the first two encounters.

These categories were found to be related to the degree to which the participant's view of himself matched his estimation of how his friends saw him. The mastery participants' views of self tended to be similar to their estimate of peers' impressions of them. In contrast, the delayed mastery group more often felt overevaluated by peers and the deteriorated group felt underevaluated by peers. These findings suggested that one's current social environment, perhaps in combination with a personality trait developed through childhood relationships with parents, led to the difficulty in coping with stress. Some later studies of affiliation have provided clues as to how such a pattern might develop.

Schachter (1959) conducted a series of experiments in which persons were allowed to wait with others (affiliation) or wait alone (nonaffiliation) after being told that the experiment would involve a painful electric shock. He was interested in the correlates of affiliation under a stressful condition (threat of shock). He did not actually shock the participants. He found that persons who had been only and first-born children chose more often to wait with others, while those who had been later born children chose to wait alone. A control group not threatened with painful shock showed no birth order differences in affiliative behavior. Earlier studies suggested that only and first-born children have higher dependency needs than later born children, and it appeared in Schachter's study that these needs were manifested in behavior under stressful conditions.

In an attempt to clarify further the nature of this process, Robertson and Dotson (1969) studied the family background, physiological reaction to stress, and affiliative behavior of high school students. After completing questionnaires on family background and participation in extracurricular activities (affiliation), the students were given an arithmetic test which appeared simple but was impossible to work in the time allotted. The situation was made more stressful by rushing the students and telling them that the test was simple. A physiological indicator of adrenaline or noradrenaline-like activity was obtained before and after the test. Among only and first-born children whose physiological reaction was adrenaline-like, affiliation was highest for those who reported parents as affectionate and indulgent. Among only and first-born children whose physiological reaction was noradrenaline-like, affiliation was highest for those who reported relatively low affection and indulgence from parents. There were no correlations of these factors among later born children.

The findings from these studies suggested a biosocial feedback theory of reaction to stress. Perhaps parents with their first child tend to be more or less indulgent and affectionate, depending on the noticeable physiological arousal of the child under stressful conditions. In turn, the degree of arousal in the child when stressed may be conditioned by the type and amount of attention he receives. A number of studies have shown that the hormonal and autonomic nervous systems are subject to external conditioning (Miller, 1969). The lack of findings for later born children could be the result of altered parental behavior because of experience with the first child, less time available for each child when a second or more arrive, or the interaction of older and younger children. It is also possible that differences between first and later born children are affected by differences in hormonal excretions of their mothers during pregnancy. Women may be more anxious in their first pregnancy. It has been shown that some hormones breach the placental barrier (Migeon, *et al.,* 1961), but it is not known what effect, if any, this has on the subsequent functioning of the child's hormonal and nervous systems.

A further set of questions leads to expansion of the theory to include possible reasons for the sustained high or low hormone production that may be a factor in certain types of diseases. What happens to a person who tends to need affiliation when stressed if he loses his close family or friends through death, moving away, or other circumstances? What happens to a person who needs to be alone when stressed if he must live in a crowded dwelling in a crowded neighborhood?

To our knowledge, no one has directly measured the affiliative needs of persons and shown the subsequent consequences when these needs are not met. It has been shown that first-born persons in isolation experiments have more stress symptoms than later born persons. In contrast, later born persons who lived in crowded slum conditions claimed to have more stress symptoms than did first-born

37

persons (Dohrenwend and Dohrenwend, 1966). In an experiment similar to Schachter's shock threat, McDonald (1970) studied the consequences of forced versus voluntary affiliation and isolation of first and later born participants. Unfortunately, he did not measure hormonal reaction. The findings indicated that first borns had greater anxiety reduction while waiting with others and later borns had greater anxiety reduction when waiting alone. Surprisingly, these results for first borns were found among those who were forced to wait with others when they had indicated a preference to wait alone, but not among those who chose to wait with others voluntarily.

Much more work needs to be done involving better, more direct, measures of affiliative tendencies and physiological as well as self-reports of reaction to stress. Nevertheless, on the basis of available evidence, we can tentatively theorize that a feedback system involving affiliative needs and opportunities for affiliation or isolation could, in some instances, account for the sustained high or low hormone concentrations over time which, in combination with noxious agents, dietary deficiencies, or genetic factors, result in disease. If a person who needs affiliation when stressed is in circumstances where affiliation is not available to him, he may be further stressed, have further increased affiliation needs, and so on. Such a positive feedback process with accompanying hormonal reaction could continue until the person finds affiliation sufficient to satisfy his needs, or he becomes ill. Similarly, the person who needs isolation when stressed, but is in a situation where isolation is impossible, may be further stressed, have intensified needs for isolation, and so on until he becomes ill.

There have been a number of retrospective studies which show a correlation between social isolation and disease (Cassel, 1970; Jaco, 1970). In one such study, involving terminal cancer patients, LeShan (1966) found the following recalled life pattern in 70 percent of the cases: "Childhood and adolescence marked by feelings of isolation; a sense that intense and meaningful relationships are dangerous and bring pain and rejection; and a sense of deep hopelessness and despair" followed by a close relationship with one person while an adult and then the "loss of the central relationship in a sense of utter despair, and a conviction that life held nothing more for them." In a comparison group without cancer, only 10 percent recalled a similar life pattern. We view such results with caution because the despair associated with impending death could alter the person's view of his life pattern.

Conversely, a number of diseases, noncommunicable as well as communicable, are found more frequently in areas where living conditions are crowded. Are persons who need isolation when stressed more likely than affiliative persons to become ill under these conditions? Clearly in the case of communicable diseases, the effect of crowding on the spread of infectious agents would have to be separated from the possible stressful effect of crowding. There is an opportunity here for some very interesting research. Studies are needed that are designed in such a way that the affiliative needs and opportunities for affiliation of persons are known prior to disease onset or their knowledge of the disease.

Another possibility for biosocial feedback that could contribute to sustained abnormal hormone production is suggested by the association of stress symptoms and self-esteem. Studies have consistently shown that self-reports of increased heart beat, trembling hands, and the like, symptomatic of an adrenaline reaction to stress, are more frequent among persons with low self-esteem than among those with high self-esteem (Rosenberg, 1965; Coopersmith, 1967). Recall that such symptoms are also found among persons with high ascribed but low achieved statuses in one study (Jackson, 1962; Jackson and Burke, 1965). Low self-esteem could lead to lack of achievement, which is stressful. Subsequently, failure to achieve could further lower self-esteem and the cycle could repeat itself until the person becomes ill as a result of the sustained hormone reaction. The process could be more complicated if illness, or the person's definition of himself as ill on the basis of his stress symptoms, contributed to further lack of achievement.

Cognitive Processes

Studies of hormonal reactions to stress generally reveal that animals show a stronger reaction than human beings. This difference could be a result of the wider variety of cognitive processes available to human beings. For example, adrenocortical hormones in women awaiting surgery to determine whether or not breast nodules were malignant were usually not as high in those who reacted to the situation in one or more of the following ways: denied the possibility of cancer, depended on religious faith, preoccupied themselves with trivial concerns, or attempted an intellectual analysis of the situation (Sachar, 1970). It is evident that these and other cognitive processes that sometimes intervene between potential stresses and the physiological reaction must be considered in research on potential means of controlling potentially harmful stress reactions (Lazarus, 1966).

The variety and complexity of the theories of cognitive processes precludes a review of them here. Like many theories in sociology, these theories suffer from a lack of adequate data to confirm or reject specific hypotheses. Vague concepts such as "weak personality structure" (Simmons, 1966) or "poor ego strength" are used to explain why some persons manage stressful events less well than others. This is partly a result of the measurement problem. In order to measure a person's thoughts, it is necessary that he or she express the thoughts; at least, with present technology this is the case. Thus, the phenomenon one is attempting to measure may have an effect on the ability or willingness of the person to give accurate information, often distorting the measurement.

A minimum set of the possible factors involved in cognitive processes are:

(1) factors involved in perception of a given situation as threatening; (2) factors involved in altering thought so as to raise or lower the activation of internal emergency mechanisms, such as hormonal arousal; (3) factors involved in the availability of options for altering the situation through some action.

At present, the organization and interaction of these factors in the brain can only be inferred from observations of behaviors, some measures of hormonal and nervous system functioning, and reports of cognition. There is widespread disagreement among scientists over these inferences.

Theories of mental diseases are based on such inferences. Schizophrenia, one of these diseases, involves the expression of bizarre thoughts and unusual behaviors, often involving social withdrawal. An external noxious agent could be a factor. For example, infection by treponema pallidum, the agent in syphilis, can lead to cognitive disorders. The concordance of schizophrenia in pairs of monozygotic (one-egged) twins, who are genetically alike, is four times that in dizygotic (two-egged) twins, who share about 50 percent of like genes. These findings suggest that a congenital physiological factor is involved in schizophrenia (Heston, 1970). There are also a number of candidates for the role of a biochemical factor in schizophrenia (Brodsky, 1970; Snyder, *et al.*, 1974). Schizophrenic thought and behavior could result from a deficiency of one or more elements needed in the brain for normal functioning, or it could result from a hallucinogenic derivative of one of the hormones or other elements in the body (Kety, 1959). If the latter is the case, the biosocial feedback processes discussed earlier could be a factor. A number of sociopsychological theories are based on observations such as the higher frequency of "damned if you do and damned if you don't" communications (*e.g.*, "I order you to disobey me"), called the double bind, in families of schizophrenics (Mishler and Waxler, 1965).

The synthesis of these theories is yet to be determined by research. However, social factors are implicated sufficiently in exposure and susceptibility to disease that there can be little doubt that sociologists will be involved in building knowledge of the systems involved. And the effects of various modes of therapy in ameliorating the problems must be evaluated in terms of their implications for social systems. But, we are getting ahead of ourselves. In the last chapter we shall return to options for research and therapeutic action, given the state of our knowledge about the structure and processes of environmental, social, and organismic systems. We now turn our attention to the effects of these systems on individual and family behavior with respect to disease prevention and help-seeking.

3
Behavior regarding health, illness, and the sick role

Maintaining health and dealing with illness are major preoccupations of many human beings. A simple "How are you?" to a friend can elicit an extended monologue about the person's aches and pains, a recent trip to the hospital, or the latest fad diet. In thinking about systems involved in human behavior toward health and illness, it is useful to distinguish among health behavior, illness behavior, and the sick role. Health behavior refers to actions people take that may lead to illness and to the avoidance of illness before the perception of symptoms (*e.g.*, Kasl and Cobb, 1966). Illness behavior includes the perception of symptoms of illness, and the actions taken to determine both their significance and treatment (Mechanic, 1962; Mechanic and Volkart, 1960). The sick role, the oldest of the three concepts, refers to the special position accorded persons with certain illnesses and the behaviors expected of them (Parsons, 1951).

Health Behavior

Although we know of no survey of the world's population on the matter, we feel safe in saying that almost everyone would prefer to avoid illness and death. However, mere knowledge of those things that contribute to the likelihood of illness or premature death does not result in systematic avoidance of these elements by most people. Undoubtedly in countries with literate populations, most people who smoke heavily, drink heavily, and travel in motor vehicles without using safety belts have at least heard that they are risking illness, injury, or death. Apparently factors other than knowledge itself intervene to prevent completely rational behavior.

Attempts to explain behavior with respect to health have focused on: 1. the information regarding illness and the actions to avoid illness that are available to people, 2. the degree to which people believe the information, 3. the degree to which they think the information applies to them personally (vulnerability), and, 4. the degree to which the needed action requires extra effort or costs in relation to the prospective effectiveness. Unfortunately, all these factors have not been studied over a wide range of potential illnesses. Therefore, we must piece together some findings from some of the better designed studies to attempt an assessment of the relative importance of the noted factors.

A person's position in various social systems can determine the amount, frequency, consistency, and accuracy of the information he receives. And, as we have noted, information entering the brain must be integrated into the organization of markers already present there. The processes whereby the information is so integrated, and in some cases is distorted, are not well understood. Therefore, health information and beliefs, usually obtained by asking people questions in surveys, are a mixture of information received from various sources, the reorganization of that information in the brain, and the ability and willingness of the respondent to recall and impart the information.

A number of surveys in the U.S. indicate that beliefs about some diseases are fairly realistic, at least in terms of the relative susceptibility of particular groups. Levine (1962) asked people to rate cancer, polio, cerebral palsy, arthritis, tuberculosis, and birth defects on a five-point scale from "much" to "little" fear. Polio and birth defects were feared more by younger people (under 45 years) than by older people, while the latter more often feared arthritis. The mentioned diseases are more immediately relevant in the respective age groups. Cancer was highly and equally feared by both groups, while cerebral palsy and tuberculosis were less, but about equally, feared by both. Jenkins (1966) found that black persons were more concerned about tuberculosis than whites, which probably is at least partially a result of the higher rate of the disease among blacks, a result of discrimination leading to low incomes and poor, crowded housing.

Levine (1962) showed that persons in whose immediate family a given disease had occurred, but who claimed to know little about the disease, were more fearful of that disease than the average person. Persons with low formal education feared all of the above-mentioned diseases more than those with more education, but those who claimed "a lot" of knowledge about disease were more fearful than those who claimed a little knowledge.

People are not completely realistic in their beliefs about diseases as shown in another survey (Kirscht, *et al.,* 1960). Half of the respondents were asked to rate their own susceptibility to a variety of diseases while the other half rated persons of the same age and sex as themselves. "Others" were consistently claimed to be more susceptible than "self" to gum disease, dental decay, tuberculosis, and cancer. Most of us apparently believe it can't happen to us.

Early research treated health behavior as uni-dimensional and emphasized its correlation with social class (summarized by Green, 1970). After showing the usual findings that preventive practices were more frequent in the middle and upper classes than in the lower classes, one group concluded that "simply reducing the financial cost of preventive health actions or confronting a person with information is not likely to change his behavior unless ways can be found to change the characteristic thinking of his social group concerning appropriate behavior patterns" (Haefner, *et al.,* 1964).

More recently, a number of types of preventive behavior were not found to be highly interrelated (Green, 1970; Steele and McBroom, 1972). In the study where the widest range of health behavior was considered, several sets of behavior were found to occur together. Each set was relatively independent of the others. Among women, the following separate sets of associated behavior were noted:

> 1. medical and dental checkups, 2. exercise, calorie limitation, and TB tests, 3. various indicators of caution such as having rain apparel, use of seat belts, knowledge of

45

first aid, and locking one's car, 4. having a will and a fire extinguisher.

Among men, only three sets were found: 1. dietary and cholesterol control, 2. medical and dental checkups, and 3. sleep and exercise.

A number of other behavioral manifestations, including the taking of polio vaccine, a concern common to a number of studies, did not correlate with other variables sufficiently to form a set (Williams and Wechsler, 1973). The diversity and inconsistency of behavior within and between individuals suggests that attempts to improve the health status of a population by changing individual health beliefs is a large and expensive, if not impossible task.

Perhaps a better way to determine the importance of attitudes and beliefs in health behavior is to consider attempts to change health behavior and the relationship of changes in attitudes and beliefs to behavioral changes. Studies of attempted health behavior change show mixed results. Many suffer from serious methodological inadequacies. Retrospective surveys which correlate claims of a given health behavior, such as obtaining a Pap smear (test for cervical cancer), with belief in the efficacy of the test prove little (e.g., Kegeles, et al., 1965). People may believe in something they have already done but that does not mean that their relevant behavior will be increased by changing their belief. We may be as likely to change our beliefs to justify our actions as we are to act on the basis of a belief.

Recognizing this dilemma, one of the authors of the mentioned retrospective study designed an experiment to test the effect of communication of "the subject's vulnerability to cervical cancer, the nature and effectiveness of cytology in detecting cervical cancer, the importance of early detection, the nature of the test, and the place and time of a special cytological clinic" (Kegeles, 1969). An experimental group of women in an urban ghetto was presented this information by a trained female resident from the same community and of their same race. A control group received a communication of similar length about nutritional anemia, with an incidental mention of the cervical cancer clinic, along with the time and place of the special clinic. Both groups were offered free babysitting and free transportation to the clinic. A significantly higher proportion of experimental than control respondents appeared at the clinic for examination. However, a visit to the clinic was not related to changes in the women's perceived vulnerability to cervical cancer, measured by questionnaire during the preceding and a subsequent interview.

Similar results occurred in an experiment that provided comprehensive medical care to children who had not previously received it. Experimental and control groups of families without a regular physician were randomly assigned from a sample of patients using a hospital emergency room. The experimental families were offered comprehensive care whereby they received both preventive health care and illness care from the same physician. The control group of families received episodic care in hospital emergency clinics, public health clinics, hospital outpatient clinics, and, occasionally, from a private physician. After three years the immunization records of the children in the experimental group were significantly better than those of the control group. However, general attitudes toward health, measured by questionnaires before and after the three year period, had not changed (Robertson, *et al.,* 1974).

These findings suggest that one need not change health beliefs or attitudes to change health behavior. Apparently the creation of medical care systems that demonstrated personal interest in the patient and conveyed normative expectations that the patient comply with recommended practice importantly altered health behavior without changing basic attitudes toward health.

Without such systems of comprehensive medical care for much of the population, alternative approaches have been attempted using such media as films and television. Most of these health education campaigns have not been rigorously tested with an adequate experimental design before being placed in general circulation. However, two recent experiments give us some insight into the possible effects of such efforts.

In one experiment, Haefner and Kirscht (1970) showed films on cancer, heart disease, and tuberculosis to three experimental groups, the films in a different order in each group. A control group met to work on a task unrelated to the films but answered most of the same questions asked the experimental group one week before, immediately after, and eight months after the films. Immediately after seeing the films, the experimental groups reported significantly higher ratings of threat of the diseases, belief in the efficacy of the recommended actions (checkups, x rays, and various changes in diet, exercise, and the like), and intentions to follow the films' recommendations. Eight months later, the experimental group claimed to have had medical checkups significantly more frequently than the control group. However, no significant difference was found in regard to having x rays or in conforming to the recommended changes in personal habits. There was a correlation between beliefs after seeing the films and subsequent action. However, change in beliefs about the diseases was not a necessary condition for action. A number of persons who showed no change in beliefs subsequently obtained checkups.

A second experiment involved an attempt to increase safety belt use in automobiles by multiple exposure to television "commercials." A pre-experimental survey showed four factors independently related to safety belt use by people whose belt use was actually observed in their vehicles. Higher formal education was most strongly related to belt use, followed closely by comfort and convenience ratings of safety belts. Having had a friend injured, but not killed, in a crash and not smoking while driving were also significantly related to belt use. Belief in the worth and safety of belts was also related to use, but this relationship no longer held when education was held constant (Robertson, et al., 1972).

On the basis of this study, six television messages were produced, each aimed at particular age and sex groupings of the population. The messages emphasized vulnerability of unbelted vehicle occupants to certain types of injuries (such as facial disfigurement). Parental responsibility for children and physician endorsement were also major themes.

A cable television system in a community where two cables were distributed in comparable areas throughout the community was used in the experiment. The homes on one cable were the experimental group, and the homes on the other cable were the control group. Over a period of nine months the safety belt messages were shown a total of 943 times, each showing on a program appealing to the relevant age and sex groupings. Persons on the control cable saw other "public service" or commercial advertising at the same time that the experimental group saw the safety belt messages. Daily observations of people in their cars were obtained a month before, during, and a month after the nine-month television exposure. The people were unaware that they were on an experimental cable system or that their safety belt use was being observed. The observed drivers were matched with experimental and control cables by tracing their license plate numbers to their addresses in motor vehicle registration files. Comparison of the experimental and control groups revealed that the messages had no effect whatsoever on safety belt use in any of the ten months of observation during the time and after the messages were shown (Robertson, *et al.,* 1974).

Although the studies are not entirely comparable because of the different kinds of behavior studied and different methods employed, apparently a key factor in changing health behavior is the degree to which the appeal to change is personalized. In the cited studies, behavior was changed most by a long-term relationship with a comprehensive medical care program or a home visit by a health worker, somewhat by a personal invitation to see a film, and not at all by viewing television messages in which no personal contact was involved. The United States has been described as an "other-directed" society (Riesman, 1950) in which behavior is more a function of the expectations of others in the environment than of firmly internalized and less mutable norms. The health behavior noted here seems to be so affected. This statement cannot be made unequivocally because the personal approach is not used as often with respect to frequently required health behaviors.

Most vaccines are necessary only once or every few years at the most. Biannual or annual medical checkups, depending on age, and semiannual dental checkups are sufficient for most people. Special instances such as prenatal care for mothers and infant care require more frequent medical visits. However, behavior such as exercise, smoking, diet control, or safety belt use requires at least daily and usually more frequent attention, often at some discomfort or inconvenience to the individual. Evidence is accumulating that approaches seeking to change behavior, particularly where the behavior is required frequently for adequate protection, have not been successful. And, even if some such approach were shown to be successful using some type of personalized behavior-modification technique, the effort and cost of applying such techniques on a mass basis for a variety of behaviors would likely be prohibitive.

49

A striking illustration of failure to change behavior was provided by an attempt to increase automobile safety belt use. In response to a Federal Government motor vehicle safety standard, cars manufactured from January 1, 1972, to August 30, 1973, for sale in the United States were equipped with a buzzer-light system to encourage vehicle occupants to use safety belts. A sensor in a given seat activated the buzzer and light when the seat was occupied by more than a certain weight, the ignition was on, the transmission was in a forward gear, and the lap belt was not extended at least four inches from its normally stowed position. Such a system is defeatable in many ways. A survey of actually observed belt use in the spring and summer of 1972 found no overall significant difference in belt use by drivers in buzzer-light equipped cars and those of the same model year but manufactured before January 1, not equipped with the system (Robertson and Haddon, 1974).

The buzzer-light system was claimed to increase safety belt use when especially equipped cars were driven for a time by selected drivers (Shaw, 1971; Perel and Ziegler, 1971). However, among other inadequacies, these studies involved personal attention to safety belt use in the form of explanation of the system in one case and administrative directives that safety belts be worn in the other, in each case introducing factors that were not present when the system was employed on a mass scale. The observed effect on behavior in the preliminary studies was apparently a result of the normative expectation that belts should be worn, not because of the mechanical device.

Cars in the 1974 model year were equipped with a system that prevented cars from starting unless belts were extended or latched. Belt use more than doubled to about 60 percent use in these cars (Robertson, 1974). However, public reaction was so strong that Congress banned the starter-lock system, and unobtrusive approaches to crash loss reduction were threatened as well (Congressional Record, 1974). Clearly there are limitations on public acceptability of obtrusive health behavior change strategies.

Illness Behavior

Illness behavior differs from health behavior in a number of respects. Once a person perceives a symptom, the threat of severe illness or even death becomes more immediate. With more severe or painful symptoms, inaction is likely to be a viable alternative for only the most spartan of us. The systems of the body are so complex and the outputs indicative of pathology occur in such a variety of combinations that even skilled physicians may have difficulty in diagnosing the site and nature of the problem. It should not be surprising that laymen occasionally engage in elaborate help-seeking for trivial symptoms while others show lack of concern over symptoms possibly indicative of serious problems.

There have been numerous theories and some data generated to explain illness behavior. No single theory has emerged to account adequately for the variety of behavior observed. We shall not review all of the available theories or research, but instead have chosen to select for discussion some studies that illustrate the types of systems involved in illness behavior.

We know the least about how the central nervous system processes and integrates inputs from other body systems that may indicate pathology. Such symptoms as pain and nausea that are not observable by other persons in the environment cannot be distinguished adequately by researchers from factors such as willingness to complain. There may be individual differences in the types of stimuli reaching the brain in the presence of comparable body states. Willingness to complain may not be commensurate with the severity of the experienced symptom. Studies of such phenomena as "thresholds of pain" are measuring unsorted combinations of phenomena.

One research strategy involves the experimental introduction of known levels of painful stimuli. However, the same levels of external stimuli are not necessarily processed in relevant body systems in the same way in different persons. Nor does experimentally induced pain necessarily simulate pain of pathological origin. Morphine usually eases the pain of disease but has little or no effect on laboratory-induced pain (Beecher, 1970). Conversely, significant proportions of persons complaining of pain or other non-specific symptoms report relief when they think they have been given an active drug but, in fact, have been given a nonactive substitute, called a placebo. Over half of the persons complaining of such diverse symptoms as headaches, motion sickness, and postoperative pain, claim relief when given placebos (Beecher, 1964).

Surgery has also been shown to have a placebo effect for

51

certain types of pain. For a period in the 1940's and 1950's the pain of heart disease was thought to be relieved by a type of major surgery. To test the value of this surgical procedure, a number of investigators, after explaining the situation to a series of patients, performed the surgery on some of the patients. They performed sham surgery on others without either group of patients knowing which operation had been done. There were no differences between the two groups in the frequency and duration of heart pain after the surgery (e.g., Adams, 1958). Whether the widespread interest in the anesthetic properties of acupuncture and other non-drug means of controlling pain will lead to better understanding of the systems involved in perception of pain remains to be seen.

A survey of hospitalized or recently incapacitated patients showed pain the most frequent initial symptom. When the respondents were asked what first brought their attention to the problem: 66 percent mentioned pain, 17 percent fever or chills, and 10 percent shortness of breath, while numerous other symptoms were mentioned by fewer than 5 percent (Suchman, 1965a). Unfortunately, a sample of persons with less serious illnesses was not obtained to determine the degree to which these symptoms are peculiar to serious ailments.

Sociologists have mainly focused on the relation of differences in perception of pain and other symptoms to ethnic background and socioeconomic status. A number of investigators (Zborowski, 1969; Zola, 1966; Croog, 1961) have found consistent results when comparing descriptions of pain and other symptoms among persons of Irish, Italian, Jewish and "old American" (usually white Anglo-Saxon Protestant) backgrounds. For example, Zborowski (1969) studied two groups of men in a veterans' hospital, one having severely painful herniated spinal discs and a second with a variety of other problems. In both groups Jews and Italians tended more often to express anxiety and other emotions and to be less precise in indicating the anatomic sites of the pain. "Old Americans" tended to be more matter-of-fact about the pain and describe its primary and secondary sites in intricate detail. The Irish patients more often denied the existence of pain. Italians were more frequently interested in immediate relief of the pain by whatever means, while the old Americans more often expected the use of technical means of diagnosis and that the problem could be cured by the techniques of modern medicine. Jews were more concerned than the other groups about the meaning of their symptoms in terms of their future health.

Zborowski speculated that these differences resulted from differences in child-rearing practices and other elements of the cultural systems of these different ethnic groups. However, the particular elements of the child-rearing systems have not been specified by empirical investigation. The type of attention to symptoms, the degree of emotional response to illness, and the modes of seeking solutions to problems are no doubt learned by children, mainly from parents.

One aspect of family structure, number of children, does account for some of the variation in the frequency of physician visits. In a random sample of families in two communities in Great Britain, Hare and Shaw (1965) found that a greater number of physician contacts for both mothers and fathers, respectively, occurred in families with a larger number of children. However, the average number of physician contacts per child was less in large families than in small families. These results were interpreted as a consequence of the strain of a large family on parents and the limitations on the time and attention the parents could give to each individual child as family size increased.

This study was replicated in a sample of low-income families in Boston with the addition of measures of the mother's perception of "strain" and religion (Robertson, *et al.,* 1967). Protestant mothers who claimed to "work under strain" reported more medical contacts when their families were larger, while those with larger families who did not report strain had fewer medical contacts. Perception of strain was higher among Protestant mothers with larger families. There was no relationship between family size and medical contacts or perception of strain among Roman Catholic mothers. At that time the value of a large family and the resulting perception of strain and medical utilization was different for Catholics and Protestants. However, when the same observations were obtained from these families 30 months later, religion and perceived strain no longer made a difference in the relation of family size and mother's use of physicians. Regardless of these factors, mothers with larger families went to physicians less often than those with smaller families (Robertson, *et al.,* 1974), a reverse of the finding in Britain. The results for children, however, were the same in both periods of the Boston study as in the British survey, fewer physician contacts in larger families.

The fact that the Boston sample was more homogeneous as to socioeconomic status but more heterogeneous in religious and ethnic groupings could account for some of the differences among parents. The differences may also arise from differences in the cost of medical care to adults in Great Britain and the U.S. As children grow older and more money is needed to feed, clothe, and house them, low-income parents with larger families may be forced to neglect obtaining treatment for some symptoms in a society such as the U.S. where medical care is costly to the individual family—unless their income is so low as to qualify them for medical care under public assistance.

Most studies of the use of medical services measure elements of only one or two systems such that the complex interplay of various systems remains obscure (McKinlay, 1972). Personal and cultural propensities toward perception of symptoms and the use of physicians, family and other group structural factors, economic barriers, and accessibility of medical care are seldom considered simultaneously in a single study. The distinction between those factors that are internal to the family or individual and those determined by economic and medical care organization is important for strategies to detect and treat illness. However, failure to consider all relevant systems, especially where they interact, can result in ineffective and even destructive strategies from both patient and medical care system perspectives.

Usually mathematical models are employed in attempts to account for large numbers of variables considered simultaneously. For example, an analysis of infant deaths in the state of New Mexico used census data, availability of types of physicians, availability of hospital beds, and percentage of births in hospitals versus other places, as possible predictors of rates of neonatal and postnatal infant death rates (Anderson, 1973). By making assumptions about which variable could or could not cause another variable, it was possible to construct equations that may show the causal paths through various social systems that increase or decrease the probability of infant mortality. The availability of physicians and hospital beds increased as a function of urbanization and increasing incomes, which resulted in an increase in births in hospitals and an associated decline in infant mortality.

The author of that study recognized that a number of factors could intervene in the process which were not considered. For example, normative expectations of the proper place for child delivery may differ by types of physicians available or by the social class of the expectant mothers. Nor can one assume that delivery in hospitals is a necessary condition for lowering the infant mortality rate. Poor nutrition, poor prenatal care, and possibly other factors related to infant mortality may be correlated inversely with hospital delivery.

The Boston study of family size mentioned earlier also showed some interesting interactions among parents' orientations toward the treatment of various types of children's complaints, the clinics' handling of the complaints, and the use of the comprehensive care clinic and other facilities (Robertson, *et al.,* 1974). Some of the families were in an experimental group receiving comprehensive care, and the others were in a control group. Before entering the comprehensive care program, the parents were more often oriented toward using a private physician for illnesses involving a high fever and toward using the emergency clinic of a hospital for injuries, although in most cases both complaints were taken to the emergency clinic. During the experiment the physicians in the comprehensive clinic usually saw children with fever in the comprehensive clinic but at times would meet the family in the emergency clinic of the hospital for an injury. Thus the physicians' behavior reinforced the mothers' preexisting orientation. Since younger children more often have illnesses involving fever and older children are more frequently injured, the older children tended to disengage from the comprehensive care program. The families bypassed the comprehensive care physician for injuries and, as a result of referral or other factors, eventually bypassed him for other complaints as well.

Families on welfare also tended to disengage from the comprehensive care program over the three years of the experiment. In their case, however, factors totally external to the program along with the personal orientations of the people involved apparently caused the disengagement. Despite special arrangements with the welfare department made for these families, some welfare workers continued to insist that the families use the local city hospital rather than the comprehensive care clinic. Also, welfare families, often without money, frequently relied on the police ambulances to transport them to medical care facilities. The police policy was to take them to the nearest facility, not the comprehensive care clinic. Thus, behavior of medical care personnel and the policies and behavior of other systems external to the family can have an effect on illness behavior in conjunction with or in addition to the orientations of the patient or his family. These intricate interrelationships of social systems which lead to differential use of medical resources by different groups are not revealed by gross correlations with demographic factors.

Peer expectations and nonmedical sources of information no doubt play an important role in decisions to use drugs or seek help not recommended by physicians, as well as to seek medical help. Perhaps the best study of a number of levels of social systems and individual orientation in relation to use of medical care was done in New York City (Suchman, 1965b). A community level factor (exclusiveness of ethnic groups), a social group factor (solidarity of friendship circles), family factors (tradition and authority), and individual factors (knowledge of disease, skepticism of medical care, and dependency in illness) were measured. Low knowledge of disease, skepticism of the value of medical care, and dependency were inter-correlated, and these factors were more frequent where ethnic exclusiveness, group solidarity, and family tradition and authority were high.

These factors, however, were related differentially to types of medical care used. Individual orientation did not correlate with type of care. A composite score of "parochialism" (where parochialism represents relatively high ethnic exclusiveness, group solidarity, and family tradition and authority) was correlated with more frequent use of private physicians rather than hospital outpatient clinics and a group health plan. This finding was interpreted as a "stronger need" among persons from more parochial groups for more informal, personalized medical care. Perhaps so, but it is also possible that the private physicians involved were a part of the relevant ethnic or social groups and that physician selection was made on that basis.

The persons termed "parochials" in the above study would

be unlikely to consult a psychiatrist or psychologist, but the use of such services also has been found to be a function of friendship circles. In this case the users were primarily persons in the higher social classes who attend the same plays, movies, concerts, and read the same books. They also generally move in the same circles as psychiatrists and psychologists. Having an "analyst" is normative, and switching to the latest "in" clinic, analyst, or analytic method is not unusual (Kadushin, 1969).

Many illnesses resolve themselves, or are not curable. If contacted, a physician can only offer symptomatic relief and emotional support assuming he is inclined and has the ability. But with some diseases, early diagnosis and treatment can mean the difference between life and death. Delay in seeking care for such illnesses is not uncommon. If found early, about half of the cases of various types of cancer can be arrested or cured by surgery or drugs. Yet only about half of this group, or a quarter of the total, present themselves to physicians and are properly treated in time to prevent death from the disease. Although a small proportion of these deaths results from physician delay in making the correct diagnosis or in referring the patient to an appropriate medical specialist, most of them occur because the patient delays to seek diagnosis or treatment (Blackwell, 1963).

The research on delay in seeking medical care for serious illnesses has produced mixed results (Kasl and Cobb, 1966), but some patterns can be discerned. Protestants are more likely to delay seeking care than other religious groups (Kutner, *et al.*, 1958), perhaps reflecting this group's greater stoicism with respect to illness as noted earlier. A study in Scotland found that almost 40 percent of cancer patients who had delayed in seeking medical care claimed to have done so because they did not consider their early symptoms to be serious enough to see a physician (Henderson, 1966). Since the early symptoms of cancer may resemble those of mild illness, some patients, particularly those unlikely to complain about any symptom, may delay through misperception of the seriousness of the symptom.

However, these apparently are not the primary reasons for delay. Even when the general tendency to seek or not seek medical care for various symptoms is controlled or when the patient suspected cancer originally, delay in seeking diagnosis and treatment is commonly found (Kutner and Gordon, 1961; Goldsen,1963). The concepts of denial and repression have been used to describe the cognitive patterns of patients who delay seeking care. Apparently, most of us are unable or unwilling to entertain consciously the thought that we might die. Paradoxically, such cognitive processes lead to neglect of curable illnesses until they are indeed terminal.

The research methods for measuring the processes whereby people repress cognitions that they will not or cannot entertain are imprecise. One method that reveals evidence of the phenomena, if not the process, is to ask people why someone other than themselves might do what they themselves had done. In the previously mentioned study in Scotland, over 60 percent of those who had delayed seeking care for cancer said that "others" delay because of "fear of what they will be told" but only 21 percent of the patients admitted that they, themselves, had delayed for that reason (Henderson, 1966). Even physicians, presumably more knowledgeable about the disease and that the prognosis need not be fatal, have been found to be about as likely as their counterparts in the lay population to delay seeking treatment for cancer (Blackwell, 1963).

A study in a large metropolitan hospital from 1968 to 1970 found similar rates of delay in seeking care among cancer patients as had been found in a similar study in the same hospital 50 years earlier (Hackett, et al., 1973). Correlates of delay such as its higher frequency among persons in the lower social classes were similar to those found in earlier studies. Once again, evidence of denial was strong. Persons with longer delays were significantly more likely to use the word "tumor" or "some other euphemism" in referring to their disease, while the word "cancer" was used more freely by those who had delayed less. A friend of one of the authors, who had a cancer successfully treated, has remarked that his friends go to great ends to avoid the word cancer in his presence. The nature and process of such normative patterns in various social groups should be investigated if we are to understand the factors that lead people to delay seeking medical care. The willingness to admit that one is sick and the willingness of his peers in the social system to invoke the norms of the sick role is perhaps an important element in the individual's use of denial as well as other forms of illness behavior.

The Sick Role

In its original conceptualization, four basic elements were said to comprise the sick role:

1. exemption from ordinary social role obligations; 2. acceptance of care from others; 3. expectation of a desire to return to health; 4. consultation and cooperation with an appropriate medical authority (Parsons, 1951).

Since many illnesses are mild and short-lived, most of these elements are probably not present for most illnesses (Kosa and Robertson, 1969). And, even in the case of serious and/or chronic conditions, some of these elements do not apply.

For the expectations that make up a role to operate generally, the members of the group must agree on the content of the role. However, one study showed considerable disagreement as to what persons with what symptoms would be considered sick. In a survey of 808 adults in New York City, Gordon (1966) found that people often applied the term "sick" to conditions with questionable but possibly poor prognosis such as severe pneumonia. However, less than a third of the respondents considered someone who had lost the use of his legs or who was deaf as sick. Gordon thus rejected the unimodal concept "sick role" and suggested that there were other roles such as an "impaired role." He found that the elements of these roles were quite different and that they varied by the socioeconomic status of the person defining the role.

While persons considered sick were expected to be dependent, persons with impairment were expected to fulfill social responsibilities, do useful work, and take care of themselves. The lower the socioeconomic status of the respondent, the more often he expressed the expectation that dependency accompanied sickness. Since persons with limited resources more often have to be at the mercy of others when ill than their more affluent counterparts, their expectations appear to reflect reality. A more in-depth study of 29 males over 60 years of age also concluded that, as reflected by these respondents, there are many types of sick roles rather than a unimodal one. Some variation was found among ethnic groups but the sample was too small to explore these differences adequately (Twaddle, 1969).

A definitive empirical study of the roles of persons with various illnesses and impairments remains to be done. Goffman (1963) has generated a number of provocative hypotheses based on his observations of the real or imagined stigma attached to persons with certain diseases, impairment, or disfiguration. The effect of role expectations on perceptions and behavior of persons labeled as mentally ill, and those who must deal with them, needs further exploration (Weinstein, 1972). One disease, alcoholism, has been shown to be anathema to most people in one survey in New Zealand. The vast majority of the respondents would not marry an alcoholic, share a room with one, rent a room to one, or work with one if they had a choice in the matter.

Over a third wanted no contacts with alcoholics whatsoever (Blizzard, 1972). The degree to which these or other expectations are perceived by the ill persons in a number of diseases, and perhaps exacerbate their conditions through stress or other factors, is worthy of more intensive investigation.

A major aspect of the roles of the sick or impaired is the relationship of these roles to physicians and other professionals in medical care systems. Before proceeding to that topic, however, it is useful to trace the careers of physicians and other professionals in order to better understand their perceptions, behaviors, and roles in the patient-professional relationship.

4
The medical profession

Someone who thinks he is ill may select from a variety of resources for help. Many continue to consult with practitioners not sanctioned by the medical profession. Faith healers, herb doctors, and cancer quacks persist. Practitioners such as chiropractors do a thriving business despite serious scientific doubts about their theory and efficacy of their treatment (Wardwell, 1972). However, the theory and treatment used by some in the medical profession is no less open to question.

The healer is faced with a suffering person whose problem he may or may not understand and for whom he may or may not have the means of relieving the suffering or restoring health. Perhaps because of this unique responsibility and its associated awe, the healer has occupied a special position in most societies. The responsibility of the healer was recognized by the ancient Greeks. Most novitiates in the medical profession continue to swear the oath of an early Greek practitioner, Hippocrates.

The professional role includes a first obligation to those the professional serves regardless of personal needs (Blau and Scott, 1962); it is now applied to persons in a number of occupations (medicine, law, the clergy, teaching, nursing, social work). The term "profession" has been expropriated by persons in all sorts of occupations, no doubt because of the special position of professionals in society. Rather than distinguish some occupations as professions and others as something else, it is more useful to define the characteristics of a professional role and examine the degree to which an occupation has those characteristics.

The norms that define a role (one such norm being the expectation that the needs of the client have first priority) are not necessarily followed by all who occupy the positions to which the role applies. Nevertheless, the formal statement of the role and the possibility of sanctions for nonconformity have at least some effect on the occupants.

Many occupations involve rather simple tasks that almost anyone can master in a relatively short time. Others involve a complex and ever-changing body of knowledge. In addition to the priority of client needs, the complexity of the knowledge involved is a primary element of a profession. And, because the knowledge is changing and often uncertain, the person in a professional role requires lengthy training to learn the knowledge that exists and also how to acquire new knowledge. Also, since the body of knowledge is vast and complex, professionals as groups have usually been able to resist extensive regulation of their activities by other elements of society that are less well versed in the knowledge.

In sum, an occupation is more like a profession to the degree that it involves an ethic of first priority service to clients; long-term training in a complex, changing, and uncertain body of knowledge; and autonomy in the application of that knowledge for appropriate clientele. Judged by these criteria, medicine is no doubt one of the most professional of occupations.

The tradition of human service which dates to the ancient Greeks remains. The official code of ethics of the profession states "the prime object of the medical profession is to render service to humanity; reward or financial gain is a subordinate consideration. . . . The avowed objective of the profession of medicine is the common good of mankind. . . . Physicians dedicate their lives to the alleviation of suffering, to the enhancement and prolongation of life, and to the destinies of humanity" (McFadden, 1967). The training period, because of the complexity of the knowledge of the human body and the techniques needed to treat it, is both long and arduous. Moreover, medicine controls the entrance into the profession as well as the content and structure of the education of its applicants. When the first medical degree was awarded in Italy in 1140, the local ruler decreed, "Whosoever shall henceforth practice medicine, let him present himself to our officials and judges and be examined by them." Medieval punishments threatened those who dared to practice medicine without the proper credentials (Calder, 1958). The medical profession continues to control the licensing of physicians and to set the standards for practice.

Elements of the Medical Profession

Once our potential patient decides to see a physician rather than some other practitioner, he faces a variety of types of physicians from which to choose. Little is known about the public's knowledge of the medical profession. In one study where general practitioners were rated by other physicians on various aspects of competence in diagnosis and therapy, no relationship was found between the physicians' incomes and the ratings of competence. This suggests that patients selected their physicians on factors other than competence (Peterson, *et al.*, 1956).

The impression gained through conversations with a non-scientific sample suggests that there is widespread confusion about the types of physicians. Many laymen do not know the difference between an internist (a specialist in adult medicine who usually has at least three years training after medical school) and an intern (a trainee in a hospital who has just finished medical school), much less the differences among the more esoteric specialties and subspecialties of medicine.

Medicine has undergone a rapid differentiation from a set of generalists to a set of specialists. At the beginning of this century nearly all physicians worked as general practitioners trained to provide direct patient care for persons of all ages and with all types of diseases. Since that time, the profession has evolved into groups of specialists who provide medical care for specific ages, or specific diseases, or who have special competence in particular methods of diagnosis or treatment. All physicians are trained in the general canon of the profession in their initial four years of medical school. Following their graduation from medical school, however, their differentiation into specialists begins with a period of specialty

63

training, usually in hospitals, that is often as long as or longer than the initial four years of medical school. The general practitioners of an earlier generation often had only one year of hospital training after medical school.

Upon completion of the specialty residency training, the student must submit to an examination by a board composed of leading members of the specialty to be certified as a bona fide specialist. The first specialty board was established in ophthalmology (concerned with diseases of the eye) in 1917; since then the number of specialties recognized by the profession has increased relentlessly. In 1971 there were 22 separate specialties with residency training requirements and examinations for certification. They ranged from specialties in nuclear medicine or colon and rectal surgery to the more traditional areas of pediatrics (care of children) and internal medicine. In addition, there are further subdivisions of medicine, with practitioners who limit their practice to even finer subdivisions. A physician, certified or not as a specialist, may limit his or her practice to specific ages and/or problems.

Even with these finer and finer definitions of the medical profession, in the foreseeable future there will remain two major divisions of medical practice. The primary care physician may have been trained as a pediatrician or as an internist, or as a family practitioner (a new specialty involving more training than the general practitioner) who cares for both adults and children, but all three of these physicians provide first-contact medical care for patients. First-contact medical care means that these are the physicians from whom the patient seeks medical care initially, who treat the usual but often minor illnesses of mankind, and who refer a patient to a specialist or subspecialist for consultation if that patient needs more specialized diagnostic or therapeutic measures. This primary care physician, whether internist, pediatrician, or family physician, is supposed to provide coordination and integration of the various facets of care for patients with more serious illnesses.

In contrast, the second major class, the consultant physicians, provide a specific specialized knowledge or skill for patients with particular illnesses or needs. In theory they act as agents of primary care physicians, who retain primary responsibility for the welfare of patients. A consultant physician's relationship with the patient is less firmly established. By the canon of ethics of the

64

profession, the consultant is supposed to be certain that the patient referred to him returns to the primary care physician at the conclusion of the consultation.

Potential patients have no professional expertise or yardsticks by which to choose physicians and, therefore, probably select their physicians on the basis of their personal qualities, their general reputation in the community, or by looking them up in the yellow pages. A physician, on the other hand, selects the consultants to whom he refers his patients. As a member of the profession he should be able to judge more accurately the ability of the consultant physician. Friedson (1960) has made the distinction between the "client dependent" and the "colleague dependent" specialties, with the inference that the more specialized the consultant, the more dependent he is upon referrals from his peers. This distinction parallels that between the primary care physician and the consultant.

Only one physician on the contemporary scene acknowledges his sole role as the provider of primary care. The family physician states openly that his job is to provide primary care for persons in families. The internist and the pediatrician, trained as specialists in the care of adults and children, in practice are likely to provide both primary and consultation care in the same setting.

In 1971 there were 310,845 physicians active in practice in the U.S., 90 percent of whom were involved in direct patient care. Sixty percent of the 278,535 physicians in direct patient care practiced in six specialty areas. General practice maintained the highest percentage of this population (20 percent), followed by 13 percent in internal medicine, 10 percent in general surgery, 7 percent in psychiatry, 6 percent in obstetrics and gynecology, and 6 percent in pediatrics (Roback, 1971). By these calculations, almost 40 percent of physicians in direct patient care provided primary care. However, the absolute numbers of physicians engaged in this activity were declining in the face of an increasing general population. For example, between 1963 and 1968 the number of active physicians providing direct patient care increased by 36,355, while there was an increase of only 2,173 physicians in general practice and internal medicine. While pediatricians also provided primary care for children, their numbers are small in relation to the numbers of children in the U.S. The number of pediatricians per 100,000 children increased from 7.3 in 1940 to 16.3 in 1961. In the same time period, however, the numbers of general practitioners providing care for children declined from 345 to 135 per 100,000 children (Weinberger and Richmond, 1970).

As a result of the decline in primary care physicians, potential patients may try to see specialists directly, in spite of the lay person's inability to choose the appropriate specialist. A pain in the chest does not necessarily mean that one needs a cardiologist (a specialist in heart diseases). As an alternative, many people have apparently turned to emergency rooms of hospitals for all complaints rather than just true emergencies. At Children's Hospital Medical Center in Boston, for example, the number of emergency clinic visits increased from about 4,500 in 1955 to about 77,000 in 1970. The vast majority of these visits were for such relatively minor complaints as routine earaches or viral illnesses which are not usually emergencies (Robertson, *et al.,* 1974).

Organized Medicine

The shortage of primary care physicians results from a number of factors, including the attempt to increase quality of medical care through specialization; the relative desirability of specialty practice in terms of income, prestige, and control of practice; and the limitation of numbers of new practitioners. To understand the profession's limitation of numbers, it is necessary to know something about organized medicine and the profession's regulation of itself.

In 1846 a group of physicians formed the American Medical Association (AMA) to upgrade the standards of medical practice primarily by influencing medical education. The AMA is now a federation of state and county medical societies. The county society sends delegates to the state society, which, in turn, sends delegates to the AMA. AMA policies are determined largely by a fifteen-man Board of Trustees elected by the House of Delegates, although policy can be proposed and ratified or rejected at semiannual meetings of the delegates.

Technically, most of the standards for licensing of physicians and charters and accreditation of hospitals and medical schools are set by state governments or by AMA councils. Because of the lack of expertise of nonprofessionals in the canon of the profession, appointees to state boards and commissions that set standards usually are recommended or nominated by the state medical societies. Thus the control of policy remains in the hands of the profession. Hospitals must be approved by the AMA Council on Medical Education and Hospitals in order for their graduates and resident trainees to be licensed. There is no doubt that the numbers of physicians in practice have been limited by these mechanisms, in spite of AMA protestations to the contrary (Rayack, 1967).

Professional standards for practice have no doubt been raised by control of education and licensing, as well as the ethical standards promulgated by the national, state, and local societies. It is also clear that policies designed to protect and extend economic and other advantages of physicians have been subsumed under the guise of medical ethics. For example, certain arrangements for salaried rather than fee-for-service practice have been condemned as "unethical practice" by AMA leaders and county medical societies (Rayack, 1967). Psychology, chiropractic, and optometry have all been limited in their encroachment into the boundaries of medical practice by the medical profession's exclusive control over the prescribing of certain drugs.

Another reason proposed for the decline in primary care physicians, and especially in the numbers of general practitioners, lies in the system of medical education. Since the medical school clinical faculties are organized into specialty departments and even subspecialty departments, the medical student is exposed during his formative educational years only to specialty consultants practicing in a university center. Moreover, success in medical school for the student is often based on competence in research or diagnosis of uncommon diseases. In addition, the patients from whom he learns in the university center more often have rare and complex maladies rather than the common complaints that make up the bulk of primary care. Finally, there is some evidence that medical students are preselected for abilities that may be incongruent with the goal of providing physicians who are comfortable with primary care practice and who can get enough satisfaction with the common, often psychosocial, problems of the general population (Haggerty, 1963). To understand the physician and his behavior, we must understand the systems which transform a young student into a mature physician.

The Process of Selection for Medical Training

Although the actual decision to pursue a medical career may occur in high school, college, or, in rare cases, afterward, many selective factors operate early in the life of the potential medical student. The decision to admit a student to medical school is based primarily on undergraduate college grades and the Medical College Admission Tests (MCAT). Those who meet minimum standards on these criteria are evaluated on personal recommendations and interviews, and extracurricular activities in college. Two characteristics are common to the vast majority of medical students: intelligence (at least as measured by grades and tests) and a compulsion to succeed, at least academically. These factors account at least partially for the underrepresentation of persons of lower class origin in medicine. One study found only 12 percent of the students in four medical schools were from the lower half of the social class hierarchy (Rosinori, 1965).

The compulsive concern with grades is evident to those who have taught or attended classes with undergraduates aspiring to medical careers. The professor who gives such a student less than an A may face a confrontation during which he is accused subtly, or otherwise, of ruining the student's prospects for a bright medical career. These sessions are particularly painful if the instructor realizes that this student is under considerable pressure from home to enter the profession. Of course, prospective medical students are not the only undergraduates under pressure from parents and others to excel in a particular career. However, the competition for entrance to medical school is particularly intense, in good part because of the limited number of available openings. This intense competition has increased in the 1970's as the sciences have begun to limit the numbers of their graduates as well.

There were 29,172 applicants for the 12,335 openings in the 108 medical schools in the U.S. in 1971, an acceptance rate of 42 percent. The intensity of the competition is reflected in the fact that the 29,172 applicants submitted a total of 210,943 applications, which amounts to an average of more than seven medical schools for each applicant (Dubé, et al., 1973). Many others who had once aspired to medicine as a career do not apply, perceiving that the race is lost.

Incompatibilities between parental and personal aspirations and between personal aspirations and personal abilities produce casualties. It is not unusual to encounter an undergraduate premed student who really wants to be a writer, chemistry professor, or engineer. He will tell you with great anguish that his family would disown him were he not to study medicine. Those with ability and strong affection or other ties to such families often persevere and become physicians but remain relatively dissatisfied in the role for the rest of their lives. Others have been known either deliberately to fail a course or two or be unable to perform because of the anxiety generated in the interaction with their families over the issue. No doubt other forms of rebellion result from incompatibility between parental expectations and personal interests. No less frustrated are those who, because of personal aspirations or family pressures, strive for a medical career but are unable to perform at a sustained high level in a sufficient number of courses to achieve it. Over half of medical school applicants eventually end up in careers outside the health care field (Becker, *et al.,* 1974).

In addition to heredity, personality, and familial factors bearing on abilities and career aspirations, broader social factors bear on aspiration and selection. Although seldom formally stated, some medical schools have banned students on the basis of religion, race, and sex. Other potential medical students do not succeed because the educational and cultural background of their families, peers, and teachers are insufficient to transmit the necessary cognitive skills and motivation.

Without question the right books, the right tutors, and the right schools increase the probability of success in the competition for grades and test scores that determine entrance to medical school. Students with affluent or well-educated parents more often have such advantages (Sheps and Seipp, 1972). Having thus been provided with a strong intellectual base, these students generally are able to compete for grades with considerably less effort than their less advantaged counterparts.

Recently, many schools have responded to community and government pressures (as well as the consciences of some of their administrators, faculty, and present students) to train more physicians by developing programs to admit some students from the lower social classes. These include summer programs to tutor prospective medical students and scholarship funds for those unable to afford a medical school career. Initially most of the students in these programs were black. As in other so-called "poverty programs," the disadvantaged who are black are more easily identified than others, and this factor, along with the crucial state of race relations, contributes to the continued underrepresentation of the white disadvantaged. The percentage of students from minority groups entering medical school increased from 4 percent to 12 percent from 1968 to 1972 (Dubé, 1973). The percentage of women increased from 9 percent to 17 percent during the same period. About 45 percent of women applicants were accepted compared with 42 percent of all applicants. The continued underrepresentation of women relative to their numbers in the population must result from factors other than actual medical school selection. We can only speculate that the medical profession continues to be perceived as discriminating or as an unacceptable role for women. The increase in women applicants indicates that, if these factors are involved, they are changing.

A little-studied aspect of the situation is the premedical advisory system in the undergraduate colleges. The premedical advisor, often a Ph.D. in one of the biological or chemical sciences, is a symbol of the colleges' recognition of this particular subsystem within its general educational system. The role of this advisor is seldom defined in detail, but, in general, he stands between the premed student and the medical school as an interpreter to the student of medical education and as an advocate for the student to the medical school. As an agent of medical education, the advisor acts as one of the filters in the pool of potential applicants to the medical school. By his definition of criteria for entrance to the profession, he may guide, support, or discourage any given student to attempt to enter medical school. This may be useful for those students who lack the minimal level of intelligence or motivation required for successful admission to medicine. However, it should be noted that the advisor has little or no first-hand experience with the process of medical education or with the attributes needed to become a successful physician.

In addition to the premedical advisor, the premedical educational system contains other subsystems that affect student aspirations. For example, informal and formal communication systems have evolved between medical and premedical education. Formal communication links exist between premedical advisors and admissions committees of medical schools in the form of visits between the two groups. Informal communications in the form of "grapevine" systems also flourish, fertilized by the premed students' avid interest in any scrap of information concerning the process of admission to medical school. Through these communication systems the premedical student is fed a more or less realistic vision of the behavior required to accomplish his goal. He is also fed a vision of the types of medical schools available to him and their salient characteristics. Even this early in his career, he is forced to make a choice about the definition of his career within the medical profession. Certain schools are defined as institutions concerned with research and scholarship, while others are defined as institutions concerned with medical practice. Certain schools have higher status than others. These stereotypes may or may not be correct in individual cases. If the student uses them as the basis for his selection, he will confirm them, thus completing the proverbial self-fulfilling prophecy.

With these several inputs from the premedical culture and feedback from the medical school itself, it is not surprising that aspirants begin early, while still in their late adolescence, to conform to a model of a physician. Certain aspects of this conformity are predictable and may be seen in almost any one of these prospective physicians. Each of them faces a prolonged period of dependency and difficult apprenticeship. In the interest of succeeding in their chosen career, premedical and medical students may postpone any action that would affect other aspects of their lives. They often delay marriage, children, and the assuming of financial responsibility well beyond the age of their peers who have not selected medicine. And, as we shall see, those who do not make these postponements usually follow different tracks than those who do.

A number of other factors are also at work to create more diversity in medical student bodies and careers. Formerly, most students came to medical school after following a rather rigidly defined premedical curriculum. Nowadays, however, more schools are accepting students with strong liberal arts majors (Funkenstein, 1967). Curricula of undergraduate departments as well as those of professional schools are highly influenced by the latest "hot" discov-

71

ery in the field. Thus, the biology major comes to medical school with an intricate knowledge of the molecular basis of cell functioning, the physics major is up on current problems in atomic particles and field theory, and the literature major on the decline and fall of the novel. However, the student who has been able to synthesize his specialized information into a body of general knowledge is relatively rare. Medical school stories of the entering student who knows a great deal about the types of cells that produce a given substance but does not know the location of the cells in the body are not uncommon (Funkenstein, 1968). Imaginative teachers are able to build on these foundations and, for some students, the synthesis eventually is accomplished.

Another source of diversity is the extracurricular milieu of yesterday's undergraduates. In the 1960's, if the entering medical student was not himself a veteran of a sit-in or some other form of "activism," he at least had the ills of modern society detailed by a "radical" student in a dormitory bull session or a sidewalk confrontation. Some students responded to such situations by joining the Young Americans for Freedom (the student equivalent of the right-wing John Birch Society), but others saw sufficient truth in the extremist rhetoric to be moved toward greater concern, if not action, with respect to the problems. Only the brightest students were able to be dedicated activists and maintain the grades necessary to gain entrance into medical school.

The campuses became quieter in the 1970's, and it is too early to assess the long-term effects of recent changes in attitudes and ideology of students and faculty. Interns and residents threatening or conducting "heal-ins" (excessive hospitalization or other treatment) for better organization and better salaries is one bit of evidence of such changes. Graduates of one medical school over the last 45 years, when asked to rate themselves on a scale from extreme liberal to extreme conservative both when they were in medical school and at the time of the study, showed little net change. About one in five claimed to be more conservative and a similar proportion claimed to be more liberal than they were as medical students (Goldman and Ebbert, 1973). Thus, the small but outspoken "activist" cohort of the 1960's may have introduced a group of physicians into the profession that will continue to press for reforms.

Many studies of medical students have been directed at

determining personality traits and other characteristics necessary to select good physicians. However, these efforts are plagued with the problem of disagreement as to the criteria for a good physician as well as problems of sampling and the precision and accuracy of personality tests and other instruments in measuring characteristics deemed desirable by whatever criteria (Bloom, 1965).

One study of medical students concludes that "such variables as the Medical College Admissions Test and premedical grade point average identify smart, achievement oriented, rather aloof individuals who know how to get good grades." They "systematically unselect with reference to such criteria as humanism" (Korman, *et al.*, 1968). Whether or not the nonscience majors, women, and disadvantaged students now being admitted are more "humanistic" is problematic. They do bring a wider variety of interests to the medical school environment, further contributing to the diversity of the milieu.

On the basis of interviews with 100 first-year medical students, one researcher classified about a third as people-oriented, and equivalent proportions respectively as science-oriented and extrinsically oriented (status, monetary reward, security). Because of sampling limitations, these proportions cannot be generalized to all medical students (Olmstead, 1973).

The Process of Medical Education

Since Abraham Flexner (1910) took American medical education to task, continual review and revision of medical school curricula has been the rule rather than the exception. New scientific discoveries and changing patterns of disease have resulted in the addition of new disciplines to the curriculum and considerable revision of the content of the more traditional courses. Physicians have found that knowledge of human biology and chemistry is insufficient to deal with many problems, the origins of which are more social than physical. Thus, psychiatry, clinical psychology, and social work have been called upon to play a greater role in medical school curricula. More recently, medical schools have looked to social scientists for answers to some of these problems. The latter trend has been accelerated by the encirclement of many urban teaching hospitals and medical schools by a predominately poor population. Medical school administrators and faculty have watched the middle class move out of the neighborhood and be replaced by the poor. Overwhelmed by the problems, as often social and economic as biological, that these people bring to the hospital, medical educators have looked to the social sciences for teaching and research that will be of aid.

Social scientists bring to the medical school a quite different orientation from that of the psychiatrist, clinical psychologist, or social worker. The latter disciplines are oriented toward the individual's adjustment to his environment. Sociologists and economists, particularly those in applied research in medical schools, see problems more often in terms of laws, policies, and organizational arrangements that work a hardship on particular segments of the population. Their recommendations for change are usually much more radical since they do not involve just the adjustment of one individual or family but involve the adjustment of large segments of the society at large. The views of such social scientists may have appealed to those students who were involved as undergraduates in various forms of activism such as sit-ins and tutorial programs in slum areas.

This is not to say that social consciousness and orientation toward social action on the part of medical students was promoted primarily by the social scientists. Indeed, their influence probably was minor when compared to the medical faculty or voices from the community. For a number of years there have been physicians teaching in medical schools whose main interest is classified under various terms such as public health, community medicine, or preventive medicine. New allies in the persons of social scientists and activist students who were also interested in community issues have helped enable these physicians to demand more time for these issues in the curriculum. Teaching physicians are more influential as far as students are concerned because medical students are prone to take more seriously the pronouncements of their medical teachers than those faculty members who do not wear white coats.

To point out these developments is not to say that medical school curricula are now primarily socially oriented. There continue to be many conservative faculty members who fight such changes with erudite logic, personal charm, and power over budgets and faculty tenure. Often they are willing to have the new types of courses offered but are, at the same time, unwilling to give up time in the curriculum allocated to the traditional basic science and clinical teaching. When some time is relinquished, however reluctantly, the same amount of work is expected from the student in the shorter time period.

The medical education system had an important input in addition to social scientists and some socially minded students that changed somewhat the organization and process of the system. The availability of poverty program funds from the government allowed some medical schools in the 1960's to become more involved in the delivery of care in the community outside their traditional role of providing in-patient and some out-patient care in the teaching hospitals. Many of the neighborhood health centers operating in large-city slums were affiliated in some fashion or another with medical schools. Although the government agencies that financed such programs placed restrictions on the degree to which medical students could participate in these efforts, the students were actively involved in the discussion of such issues as community control, the relationship between physicians and lower-class patients, and similar problems. While students were sobered by the complexity of the social and economic problems of families in the inner-city slums, many were at the same time incensed that the society could be so inhumane as to allow such conditions to persist. As one particularly sensitive community-oriented faculty member stated "when even the most aloof student talks to an eight-year-old black child from the inner city, he is hooked."

Conservative faculty members and occasionally even a socially minded medical teacher expressed concern that some students were emphasizing social and economic problems to the exclusion of gaining the basic knowledge and clinical skills that will be necessary for them to perform the traditional healing role of the physician adequately. Indeed, students were occasionally frustrated by a patient who demanded less attention to social and psychological issues and more attention to a cure for the given physical problem at issue. Insecure students interpreted such situations as personal rejection and withdrew to the biochemistry laboratory. Most, however, were bright enough and emotionally mature enough to handle the somewhat inconsistent demands of various faculty members, peers, parents, and patients and perhaps developed a more realistic view of the world and their role in it than the generations that preceded them.

Available studies of the relationship of medical students to the faculty and to one another preceded these trends and emphasized student adaptation to the medical school environment. Recent changes have not been so radical as to change the basic outlines of a curriculum that has been common in schools in the U.S. for the past fifty years. Basically the student in the first two years of his education will become immersed in the scientific basis of medicine. The biological sciences, which form the basis of current understanding of the human organism, will be taught to him in more or less detail, and he will be expected to master and gain a working knowledge of basic biological and pathological processes. Most of these first two years will be spent in academic activity in classrooms and laboratories. Even in the most liberal and innovative schools, little time will be spent with patients. In contrast, during the last two years of his medical school education, the student will spend most of his time with patients and physicians learning about the diagnosis and treatment of disease in individual patients in the hospital ward and clinic.

Any professional educational process includes several elements. In the course of his education the student must learn facts, develop skills, and acquire certain attitudes, norms, and behavior patterns. These latter elements of professional education might be called the culture of medicine. The process of his initiation into this culture is called the professionalization of the physician.

The process begins immediately as the student begins to test his expectations of his medical education with its reality. He is likely to begin with the conviction that he must learn it all because it is all important to his primary goal of caring for patients. Two realities confront him at once. The amount of information is staggering, and it becomes quickly obvious that no one can master it all. Secondly, the validity of that information changes rapidly, and, more importantly, the information is not complete. In short, within weeks of beginning his medical education, the student must lose some of his idealism in order to survive. He must select the priorities for his learning based on his own inexperience and judgment, or he must find sources within the educational system to guide him. His choice is clear, and he actively begins to seek clues from his professors to direct him.

76

One obvious feedback mechanism is the examination. The student quickly learns that to survive he must pass his examinations and that the examinations will be concerned with those issues considered important by his instructors. In effect the examination process says to him: "You must learn what we think is important. You may engage in an independent course of study but you must also master these elements of the profession." We have already discussed the fact that a student's test-taking ability has gotten him this far. He begins to expend at least some energy calculating and analyzing his professors in the interest of his survival. If he masters the process of facing the uncertainty of scientific knowledge and of selecting from an overwhelming amount of information, it will hold him in good stead. Part of his future as a physician includes both of these elements. He will as a physician be forced to live with uncertainty, and he will as well be required to select quickly from a multitude of tasks those which must be done first and those which can take second priority (Fox, 1957).

The student also begins his medical career facing death, and he must begin immediately to reassess his attitudes toward life and death. As he walks into the dissecting room to begin his course in human anatomy, he finds the cadaver, the corpse, that he must dissect. Death is often a taboo subject in society, and the student's early intimacy with his cadaver establishes his selection by the society as one who has special status. Moreover, he must begin a process of emotional detachment in order to deal with the grim reality of that embalmed corpse. One human being cannot dissect the anatomy of another, albeit dead, human being without establishing some emotional control. This emotional control will also often be necessary for the student after he becomes a physician if he is to be effective in caring for patients.

The student thus begins in his first year of medical school to face three elements of the culture of medicine, uncertainty of knowledge, need for priorities, and the meaning of life and death. Over and above what he brings from his past and in terms of his own personality, he must work to resolve these issues in the course of his professionalization. One of the ways open to him, as already indicated, is the rather simple feedback loop of compliance to his mentors' positive or negative reinforcement of particular answers and behavior.

Studies of medical students in particular phases of their

training have noted that students often become cynical (Eron, 1955; Becker, *et al.,* 1969). Whether this is primarily a way of handling psychologically the reality of death, priorities, and uncertainty of knowledge, or the reaction to the difference between idealism and reality (Coombs and Boyle, 1971) is not clear. A more recent study comparing social concern of medical students as freshmen and again as seniors found that they were more socially concerned in their senior than in their freshman year (Perricone, 1974). Another study comparing students' attitudes at graduation with their attitudes four years later showed a remarkable decrease in cynicism, particularly among those physicians whose work involved intensive interaction with patients (Reinhardt and Gray, 1973). Either those physicians who resolve the difference between idealism and reality are more likely to follow a career involving more direct patient care or direct patient care tends to reduce cynicism. This is not to underrate the problem during the educational process. Explosive situations, bitter feelings, and diversions from the primary task of education have been found to be particularly intense when the goals and perceptions of students and faculty are widely divergent (Bloom, 1971).

Although some of the factors affecting students and faculty are known, the process of medical education is still largely viewed as a black box. We know some of the characteristics of students, faculties, and facilities that form the input and we are learning more about the output in terms of eventual medical careers, but the inner processes of medical schools are worthy of much more study. For example, the dropout rate is lower in schools that have "higher total expenditures, greater proportion of out-of-state students, greater degree of intrinsic motivation reported by their students, and higher mean scores on the Science subtest of the MCAT and the EPPS Achievement scale" (Sanazaro, 1965). It is how these inputs mix to produce the results that is not well understood.

Specialty Training

Once accepted by a medical school, the student's chances of obtaining an M.D. degree are excellent, varying from 85 percent to 95 percent in a given school, depending on the above-mentioned and perhaps other factors. His eventual career in terms of specialty and practice is influenced by his personal inclinations related to his background, his financial and family situation, and his acceptance for post-doctoral training in a hospital.

Hospital residents in particular specialties have a number of more or less distinguishable social and other characteristics. Those from less economically advantaged families tend to aspire to the more prestigious specialties such as surgery. Those in psychiatry are more often unmarried and Jewish, while those in obstetrics are more often married and Roman Catholic (Kritzer and Zimet, 1967). Those in psychiatry less often have concentrated in science as undergraduates and as medical students. Students who were children of physicians more often tend eventually to enter the specialty in which they were interested as students, possibly a result of earlier knowledge of the profession (Geertsma and Grinols, 1972).

Most students do not decide on a specialty until during or after medical school. Since few general practitioners are invited to teach in medical schools or teaching hospitals, the decline in numbers of physicians in general practice may be explained partially by the lack of such career models in the student's experience. To counter the loss of primary physicians, increasing input of federal funds to support training of primary care physicians has begun. One study suggests that the recent addition of a department of family practice to their medical school may have resulted in a change in the career patterns of some of their students toward family practice. Moreover, according to the AMA, a two percent increase in family practice residents occurred in 1970–1971 (Oates and Feldman, 1974).

In the past general practitioners have tended to be older and more often married when in medical school. They were more often from small towns and rural areas, and they received less encouragement from parents, teachers, and spouse (when married) to become specialists. Most went to public schools, whereas more specialists attended private schools (Lyden, *et al.,* 1968). One survey of 200 medical students' attitudes toward rural practice indicated that the student's background and particularly the student's wife's background correlated with plans for career in a rural area. Also there was a strong relationship between an interest in family practice and a career in a rural area (Taylor, *et al.,* 1973). Thus, a combination of family background, schooling, and situational factors contributed to the choice of career.

For those who choose a popular specialty, such as surgery, the competition for a residency in a prestigious hospital is almost as intense as the competition to enter medical school. In consultation with parents or spouse, faculty sponsors, and peers the medical student ranks hospitals in order of preference, and hospitals do the same for students who have applied. A national matching program has been developed that matches the students and hospitals to optimize the preference of both parties.

Residency training has been studied less than medical school training, but recent work has focused on this important phase of professionalization. About one-third of the hospitals with residency programs are not affiliated with medical schools. Case studies of university-affiliated and unaffiliated hospitals suggest some remarkable differences (Mumford, 1970; Miller, 1970).

Interns in one large urban, university-affiliated hospital were introduced to various department heads who made prepared speeches about the traditions of the hospital and the role of each department. Medical and lay staff were distinguished by the ubiquitous long white coat on the former. The rank of members of the medical staff was evident in meetings by seating position and mode of participation in discussion of cases. Formal and informal rules were transmitted, sometimes subtly and sometimes directly. Cases involving unusual diseases and reactions to therapy were the "interesting" ones, and the admission of too many routine cases was frowned upon. Charts were regularly checked by senior residents and mistakes were noted, often in the presence of peers. Outside work in community hospital emergency rooms and the like, to supplement income, was discouraged (Mumford, 1970).

The departmental differentiation and proliferation of formalized statuses, roles, norms, and performance standards found in this hospital tend to accompany an increase in size in any organization. This is called bureaucratization. A subsequent chapter will include a discussion of the implications of bureaucracy for the training and practice of professionals.

In a study of a small community hospital much less bureaucracy was found than in the university hospital. New interns found less formal relationships among staff. Few white coats were in evidence, and people were judged more on the basis of their personality than on their position or competence. Charts were not reviewed formally, and the intern had more independent responsibility for individual patient care. Good relations with and service to the community were emphasized in meetings, formal and informal.

Interns in both university-affiliated and community hospitals have one common advantage over their counterparts in earlier decades, better pay. From 1958 to 1968 the salary for a new intern increased from $100 per month to $433 per month in the community hospital and $143 per month to $375 per month in the university hospital (Mumford, 1970). While hardly commensurate with the training and responsibility of these young physicians, this increase in salaries has partially removed many from the dependency and, in many cases, abject poverty of former interns and residents.

A hospital is a busy place, and many have perennial shortages of personnel. The resident must do a great amount of what is called "scut work," drawing blood for laboratory analysis and the like. There is little time for reading, and some residents become fearful of never being able to keep up with their fields. They develop the tactic of learning from whomever they can, whenever they can (Miller, 1970). Some tend to rely more and more on their individual experience with particular patient histories and symptoms. If their eventual practice contains mostly cases similar to those with which they became familiar at this time, these physicians may perform adequately. However, the impersonal atmosphere of the large bureaucratized hospital and the emphasis on "interesting disease" may leave many able to perform little more than a limited technical function in the physician-patient relationship. As we shall see in the next chapter, the physician-patient relationship involves more than the application of technology.

5
The physician-patient relationship

We have now introduced the important elements of the ultimate subsystem of the medical care system, the patient and the physician. It is clear from the foregoing discussions that there is no "typical" patient or "typical" physician. Each individual is a unique combination of biological and social elements which evolve over time. Yet subsets of people have many common characteristics, and the interaction of people both within and between such subsets usually is highly stylized as well as normatively regulated.

The process of interaction is difficult to measure accurately and precisely. The presence of an observer, a camera, or whatever measuring device may alter the interaction processes resulting in a distorted view of the processes. The problem can be solved by the use of hidden observers, cameras, or tape recorders, but the ethics of such means are so questionable that they are used seldomly. Thus we must again resort to the black box analogy. We know something about the inputs and outputs of physician-patient interaction, but inferences about what actually takes place between the two in the physician's office or the hospital ward are seen only through a glass darkly.

The Setting

As we have seen, different types of physicians and patients are found in different settings. A physician who has practiced for years in a small town is likely to know at least two generations of patients in families. Although he is often an older general practitioner with less technical training than his specialist colleagues, he does know the social and cultural background of many of his patients. He may or may not be skilled in dealing with tabooed subjects such as death, sex, and alcoholism, but he at least knows much of the history of his patients.

The physician in the city is more likely to be younger and, therefore, has more current training. Primary care physicians in large city and suburban areas are more likely to be internists and pediatricians. Because of the diversity and complexity of social systems in urban areas, these physicians may not have the advantage of intimate knowledge of particular social subsystems from which their patients come.

Consultant physicians who see patients by referral may see a patient so infrequently as to be unaware not only of the patient's social system but his personality as well. The intern or resident in an emergency room, in small as well as large cities, usually sees a patient only once. Furthermore, these patients come from a wide variety of ethnic and social class backgrounds, some of which are totally unfamiliar to the physician. Therefore, any physician as he begins to deal with a patient faces not only the problem of physical diagnosis based on the patient's history, physical examination, and laboratory results, but also with his uncertainty about the accuracy of the history and report of symptoms as well as the social background and personality of the patient. Such knowledge can be gained only in time.

As Plato noted, the setting and the type of patient may affect the mode of diagnosis and treatment. In a society of slaves and free men, there were also slave doctors and free doctors. Slave doctors "never talk to their patients individually, or let them talk about their own individual complaints. The slave doctor prescribes what mere experience suggests, as if he had exact knowledge; and when he has given his orders, like a tyrant he rushes off; . . ." The free doctor in contrast, "carries his enquiries far back, and goes into the nature of the disorder; he enters into discourse with the patient and with his friends, and is at once getting information from the sick man, and also instructing him as far as he is able, and he will not prescribe for him until he has first convinced him . . ." (Plato, Jowett translation, 1937). Excepting the slave status, these descriptions characterize the crowded emergency rooms and some middle-class office practices, respectively, of today.

The physician is trained, when seeing a patient for the first time, to interview the patient in order to obtain a complete history of the patient's present and past illnesses. This history which the physician has learned in medical school has a rather stylized format —beginning with the patient's chief complaint, that is, what is causing the patient to see him on that day and progressing through the patient's history of the present illness, the past medical history, the family and social history. Once the physician has taken this history, he examines the patient physically, looking for physical signs of illness. The examination is also stylized and compulsive, beginning at the head and ending at the feet.

On the basis of the information gained through his history and physical examination, the physician formulates a hypothesis of what is wrong with the patient which he calls a diagnosis. Based on this diagnosis, he formulates a plan of action.

Depending on his social background and his experience with physicians, the patient arrives with certain expectations. If he has established a mode of interaction with a physician whom he has seen a number of times, he at least knows what to expect, although he may not find the interaction totally satisfactory. If he is seeing a physician for the first time, his anxiety over perceived or potential illness may be exacerbated by lack of familiarity with the setting or style of the physician. If he has had to wait for hours in a crowded office or emergency waiting room, his anxiety may be coupled with anger. However, in the presence of the authoritative figure, the physician, the patient may not be able to express his anxiety or his anger. George Bernard Shaw wrote:

> When your child or your wife is dying, and you happen
> to be very fond of them, or even when, if you are not fond
> of them, you are human enough to forget every personal
> grudge before the spectacle of a fellow creature in pain or

85

peril, what you want is comfort, reassurance, something to clutch at, were it but a straw. This the doctor brings you. You have a wildly urgent feeling that something must be done; and the doctor does something. Sometimes he kills the patient; but you do not know that; and the doctor assures you that all that human skill could do has been done. And nobody has the brutality to say . . . 'You have killed your lost darling by your credulity.' (Shaw, 1966 edition).

Communication

The physician-patient relationship might more precisely be defined as a communication system. Any communication at its most elemental level can be defined as the transmission of a message, in the form of information, ideas, or emotions from one person to another. While the modes of communication are myriad, the communication between a physician and a patient is largely in the format of a face-to-face conversation.

Any communication system includes messages, senders, and receivers as elements. The message must be coded into a form that can be transmitted from sender to receiver. In the communication between physician and patient the codes used in the system are of two types, verbal and nonverbal. Verbal codes are the language used by the sender; what he says. Nonverbal codes, more subtle, are found in the appearance and actions of the sender of the message.

If both transmitter and receiver were always in perfect working order and both clearly transmitted and received messages with the high fidelity of a four-channel stereophonic set, our discussion of the relationship might end here and the research of a number of sociologists and psycholgists would be redundant. However, these human transmitters and receivers are not produced on an assembly line and are even more complicated than our latest wonders of the electronics world. We must therefore consider the potential distortions of communication in the system.

This system may not work for many reasons. There may be an incompatibility between the schema of the receiver and that of the transmitter. The communication may contain unstated assumptions that are not clear to the receiver. The receiver may have a limited capacity, which may be overloaded or turned off, blocking all incoming messages. There may be static on the circuit from the environment, which impedes the transmission of the message. The message itself may be confused in its conception or presentation, and finally, there simply may not be communication facilities available (Parry, 1968).

The schemas in the brains of the physician and patient must largely be treated as black boxes. In the boxes are all the attitudes, values, and habits of perception that have evolved in the individuals' interactions with social and cultural environments, in short, organization of markers in the brain that have developed from previous experience and that will affect the reception of new information. The less the congruence of the schema of the physician and the patient, the more difficult their communication. If the receiver and the transmitter use different codes for the same message, obviously the reception of the messages are going to be garbled. If the physician and the patient do not perceive the world in a similar fashion, then they will have difficulty understanding one another. For example, if an Eskimo were suddenly transported to the Park Avenue office (a posh address) of a physician in New York, the communication between the two would be at least impeded, since their language, experience, and view of the world would be entirely different. A patient from a lower-class neighborhood in the Bronx might find equivalent difficulties on Park Avenue.

Social class is one of the commonly cited factors as a barrier in the physician-patient communication and relationship. While there is not a large body of empirical evidence, there is evidence that the difference in the social class of patient and physician will impede their communication. Psychiatry is a branch of medicine that has particularly emphasized communication as a therapeutic tool. Its traditional hypothesis has been that the process of talking with a psychiatrist will provide the patient with insights that will improve the patient's psychological symptoms. The validity of the hypothesis aside, a number of workers have found that psychiatrists have selected traditional "talking therapy" for their middle-class patients, with whom their communication is easier because they share schema, and have more often selected various forms of shock or drug therapy for their lower-class patients, with whom communication is more difficult. While there are many possible reasons for these findings, the incongruity between the schema of the physician and patient and the resulting difficulty in communication must contribute to these differences in methods of psychiatric therapy (Hollingshead and Redlich, 1958; Brill and Storrow, 1960).

Another bit of evidence of the barrier of social class differences between physician and patient comes from the organization of medical care. We will discuss this issue in more detail later, but without question there is a two-class system of care in the U.S. as well as other countries, one for the middle and upper classes and one for the lower social classes. There are historical and economic reasons for this form or organization, but one reason must be the difficulty of the middle-class physician in communicating successfully with patients from a social class with which he has had little or no experience. Indeed, in the experiments in medical care for low-income groups based upon the assumed model of personalized middle class care, developed in the 1960's, it was quickly recognized that indigenous workers from the lower social classes were needed to interpret for the physician the schemas of their lower-class patients (Geiger, 1967; Banta and Fox, 1972).

A second problem in physician-patient communication is the hidden agenda. If the real motives or assumptions of the sender are unclear or unknown to the receiver, the message may be misinterpreted or completely unintelligible. In legal terms the relationship between the physician and the patient is a contract. A contract, written or unwritten, is an understanding or agreement between parties of rights and duties. The contract between the physician and the patient is usually unwritten. At times it may be unclear, because both parties have begun the contract with different assumptions about their rights and duties.

Certain general norms concerning the roles of the physician and the patient have been described by sociologists. The physician is expected to treat all patients according to scientific and medical standards whether he likes the patient or not. He is expected to be an expert in matters of health and disease. He is supposed to be emotionally neutral and detached from his patient and at the same time place his patient's welfare above his own concerns. The patient, in contrast, is expected to be freed from some of the responsibilities of adult life depending on the severity of his illness which is defined by the physician. He is expected to cooperate with the physician to get well. The physician becomes an agent of social control, validating the illness of the patient and controlling his return to the responsibilities of adult life (Parsons, 1951).

This basic model of the relationship has been elaborated and discussed by medical sociologists since the early 1950's. Unfortunately, little empirical research has appeared to validate the degree to which physicians and patients actually adhere to these norms either in their attitudes or behavior. Observations of patients and physicians on a hospital ward have suggested that the physician is caught in the dilemma of showing concern for the patient while maintaining enough emotional detachment for proper treatment (Fox, 1959). Emotional overinvolvement with a patient may result in impairment of the physician's ability to make decisions and the neglect of his other patients. Too much detachment may result in the physician's failure to listen to the patient and adequately communicate information essential to the patient's health.

The social control aspect of the physician's role gives him considerable power in this situation. The physician may be a stable, supportive figure upon whom the patient can lean, if he cooperates with the physician. If he is trying to get well, the patient may be allowed to express feelings and exhibit behavior not usually countenanced. The physician can manipulate rewards and punishments to control the patient's behavior. The physician may withhold his full responsiveness from a non-cooperative patient and, in some situations, has control over authorization of the patient's absence or return to school or work. He also has the right to terminate the contract.

One study of physicians in a community of considerable size suggests that the physician gains satisfaction and sees his role as taking personal responsibility for patients. He enjoys the intellectual satisfaction of solving his patient's problems, and takes pleasure in helping and caring for people. He also enjoys maintaining personal and professional standards and his status in the medical and general community. He does not like restrictions on his professional independence. Finally, he dislikes not being paid by a patient (Ford, *et al.*, 1967). Patients, in contrast, want a physician who is medically competent, but compassionate and communicative (Koos, 1954).

These elements may be more or less present in the agenda

89

of a patient or physician during any encounter. It is possible, indeed perhaps frequent, that the two persons do not agree on the details of the contract. If the disagreement remains unstated, communication is blocked or impeded. For example, if the physician views his job as one involving the care of not only the physical but also the emotional status of the patient and the patient enters the physician's office wanting only a cure for his athlete's foot, the physician's questions about his sexual adjustment will, at least, startle him. The communication between these two may begin to resemble the old vaudeville routine of "Who's on first and what's on second." Similarly, many patients enter the examining room under the guise of a complaint which the physician may view as trivial and unworthy of medical attention. The patient may really want to talk about an emotional or family problem but does not know how to broach the subject. In one study of over 12,000 patients in 15 general practitioners' offices, about one in five brought up emotional or family problems (Brown, *et al.*, 1971). The number who wished to do so but did not know how is unknown.

The agenda may not only be hidden, it may not be perceived consciously. Without becoming entangled in the intricacies of psychoanalytic theory, two premises of Freud must be understood. The unconscious, according to his theory, is a composite of memories, experiences, and attitudes (the black box again) that have been imprinted in a person's central nervous system and of which the person is unaware. These hidden markers influence behavior that may seem irrational unless the unconscious material is uncovered. Transference, the concept relevant to our considerations of the physician-patient relationship, is defined as an unconscious displacement upon the physician by the patient of feelings and attitudes that he held previously for his parents or other important persons in his past. Countertransference, not surprisingly, is the reverse of this process, that is, a displacement by the physician onto the patient of feelings related to his own past. While precise validation for this formulation is lacking because of the black box problem, the notion is one reasonable explanation for the negative reactions of some persons toward others when they interact.

The physician is in a position of power and authority relative to the patient. If the patient's unconscious markers of experience with powerful and authoritative figures have been favorable,

90

he may have less difficulty communicating with such persons as physicians than someone whose experience has been otherwise. The concept of transference has been used to explain some patients' regression to childlike behavior and dependency during an illness. The physician who has had unfavorable experiences with dependent, childlike people may dislike such a person and react accordingly without understanding his feelings or action.

Another impediment to any communication system is the limitation in the capacity of the receivers of the system. Receivers may be turned off or overloaded, resulting in lost or garbled messages. The literature on death and mourning provides an example of an off-switch phenomenon. Patients who have been told that they have a serious or fatal disease often hear only that first statement of the physician. The physician may be unaware that any further explanation must await the patient's processing of that information before proceeding with any other information, instructions, or support. The patient's receiver of information in essence has been turned off and until it is again switched on, essential information can be lost (Lindemann, 1944; Solnit, 1959; Kubler–Ross, 1970).

Some examples of circuit overload are less dramatic. Either the patient or, more usually, the physician may provide so much information to the other that the receiver cannot process any further input. The physician often verbally gives the patient a detailed set of instructions that the latter does not understand. The instructions sound like the directions given at the gasoline station when you are lost in a strange city. You hear the first step and, if blessed with a good memory, the second; after that your receiver is overloaded and you hear no more. The patient, like the lost stranger, may be hopelessly lost unless someone intervenes by some technique that will relieve his receiver overload (Fink, *et al.,* 1969).

Even if transmitted at a receivable pace through a wide-open receiver, the code may not be understood. The message from the transmitter to the receiver may be in a code that is confused or unintelligble. Obviously, a prerequisite for communication is a common language. Physicians, particularly in urban centers, are often confronted with patients who literally do not speak the same language as themselves. In these situations both patient and physician must resort to a second type of code, nonverbal communication. The frustration of both is obvious, and the difficulty in communication is enormous. There are other problems in language that are matters more of semantics than of translation. For example, the physician attempting to deal with a patient from the black ghetto may find himself learning an argot of which he is completely ignorant. In fact, there are emotional lexicons transmitted from physician to physician and designed to assist the physician in a new locale to understand the language of the community.

These problems in language are related to the issue of social class already considered. George Bernard Shaw's *Pygmalion* or its more contemporary version, *My Fair Lady,* explores this problem with more wit than usually exhibited by either physicians or sociologists. As Shaw tells us, the cockney dialect of the lower social classes of London often is not intelligible to the outsider. So too the physician and patient from different social classes in any country may have problems in the presentation of their messages to each other.

There is one other problem in presentation that occurs regularly. Physicians at times explain matters to their patients in medical jargon, which is a language foreign to the patient of any social class. Tape recordings of physician-patient conversations in which the physician is explaining the patient's condition reveal enormous if nondeliberate use of technical language that the patient would have no reason to understand. One study of mothers' understanding of what the physician said about their childrens' illness and treatment revealed the following interpretations: " 'Lumbar punctures' (a technique to remove fluid from the spinal canal) were thought to drain the lungs, 'meningitis' (an infection of the brain) was understood to be located in the throat, and the 'incubation period' was interpreted to be the prescribed time for the patient to stay in bed. . . . one mother told the interviewer the doctor said that they would 'admit her for a workup—whatever that means.' It was not clear to her that this meant hospitalization of the child." (Korsch, *et al.,* 1968). One writer has noted the case of the patient who called a physician friend for an interpretation of the instructions another physician had given her. She was too embarrassed to explain to the physician giving the instructions that she did not understand them (King, 1962). On the other hand, the patient who understands the jargon may resent an oversimplified explanation. In any case, communication in a code that the patient does not understand is useless at best and can be dangerous when it results in the wrong treatment regimen for a serious illness.

There are two final problems in communication that must be considered. Noise on a communication circuit will certainly impede the transmission of messages. Such noise may be caused by many factors. The receiver may be receiving or processing messages from multiple sources and be unable to process them all. If the physician has just that morning been asked for a divorce by his wife, he is likely to be so distracted as not to be able to hear his patient. If the patient has brought his wife with him, there may be no way he can get a message to his physician because of the environmental static coming from that direction.

Finally, the physician may face a situation in which there are no communication facilities available. The unconscious patient is the paramount example of this type of barrier. The physician in this instance loses one of his primary tools of diagnosis and must rely upon a determination of the patient's physiological state independent of communication. The pediatrician dealing with preverbal children also develops some considerable skill in determining the cause of a child's problem on the basis of, at most, primitive nonverbal clues to pain and illness.

Outcome

Now that we have noted some aspects of the systems that form the elements and process of the physician-patient system, we must ask whether it makes any difference. What is the outcome of this system? Since, in general, it is easier to measure outcome than to look inside the black box of the process, there are more data in this area. The first has to do with the concept of the advantage of continuity of medical care. Given the problems in communication noted above, the hypothesis that the patient seeing the same physician over time will facilitate communication and thus improve the outcome of medical care has long been entertained. We have defined the primary physician as one who is first contacted by the patient and who not only treats most of the patient's illnesses, but also provides a coordinating role in the event of a need for consultation with other physicians. Medical care experiments done in low-income groups during the past decade seem to support the validity of the usefulness of a continuous physician-patient relationship.

In a controlled experiment of pediatric care for low-income families in Boston, it was found that those families in the experimental group provided with a stable relationship with a physician had fewer hospitalizations, fewer broken appointments with the physician, lowered use and cost of laboratory tests, a higher degree of satisfaction with their care, and a higher rate of immunizations and other preventive health indices than did the control group families who did not have a sustained relationship with a physician (Robertson, *et al.,* 1974). A series of studies on the impact of a similar comprehensive care program in Rochester, N.Y., found a decrease in the use of the emergency rooms of the local hospitals and that its users had fewer admissions to those hospitals. Presumably, these results can be ascribed to the introduction of a stable relationship with a physician for low-income families who had no access to this type of care previously (Klein, *et al.,* 1973; Hochheiser, *et al.,* 1971).

By contrast, a study in a similar program in Boston, Massachusetts showed that the program had little or no effect on the use of the emergency room of a nearby hospital (Moore, *et al.,* 1972). Differences in patients, services, or other factors could account for the differences in the two cities, but specific reasons are unknown.

In a controlled study of a comprehensive care clinic based in a university hospital, the families with their own pediatrician expressed greater satisfaction with their care than the control families without a regular pediatrician. In addition, the physicians in the experimental program expressed greater satisfaction and less frustration than their colleagues who did not have a relationship with their patients in the clinic (Becker, *et al.,* 1972a).

Comparable controlled studies of the medical care patterns of the middle class are not available. It is therefore difficult to determine whether these rather consistent findings would also occur where original social class-related barriers to physician-patient communication are less marked.

A second type of research has concerned itself with the issue of the patient's compliance to medical advice and therapy. The outcome commonly studied is the compliance of the patient to the physician's directions for taking drugs. For example, parents of a child with a streptococcal throat infection are instructed to give the child penicillin for a full ten days to ensure that the drug has completely eliminated the microbe. Yet it is not unusual for parents to cease giving the drug when the child feels better, which usually occurs in less than ten days (Bergman and Werner, 1963). While it is obviously a multivariate problem of motivation, there are a few studies that have been sophisticated enough to tease out some of the factors involved in the patient's decision to take his medication faithfully and as the physician prescribed. Two studies of mothers of children, one in the clinic setting and one in a private practice setting, found that mothers who saw the same doctor regularly were more likely to maintain a penicillin regimen for their children (Charney, *et al.,* 1967; Becker, *et al.,* 1972b).

At least one factor in the outcomes of a continuous relationship with a physician is presumably the improved quality and understanding in messages communicated. One should not oversimplify this explanation, however. Undoubtedly, free, open, and mutually understood communication influences the patient's and physician's behavior, but the behavior of patients and physicians is generated by many factors and it would be naive to assume that such a communication system will always produce favorable outcomes.

In almost all human interaction each individual is attempting to manipulate the other person for some gain, approval, physical improvement, relief from boredom. A continuous relationship may be mutually rewarding, but it is not always so. In one of the experimental comprehensive care programs for low-income families, for example, there were incidents that illustrated that continuity is not always in the best interest of physicians or patients. A telephone call by a child early Sunday morning, claiming that the mother was out and asking for a house call, irritated the physician and resulted in a punitive attitude toward the mother. A public health nurse encountered a mother who had not been to the clinic for a number of months and upon asking why, learned that the woman had become pregnant illegitimately and was ashamed to face the people in the clinic who had been "so nice" to her (Heagarty and Robertson, 1971). Thus the noted advantages of a continuous relationship between patient and physician should be viewed as net gains, and not as a utopian state in which each is completely satisfied.

The nature of the physician-patient relationship is not

determined simply by the social background, personalities, and communication of the participants. The distribution of populations of physicians and patients and the location and organization of the offices, hospitals, and other facilities influence access to medical care and have considerable influence on continuity, communication, and outcome of the physician-patient relationship. We must forge ahead to these issues.

6
The medical care system

It has become commonplace to describe the delivery of medical care in the United States as a "nonsystem." What this somewhat pejorative term means is that there is little or no overall formal planning and organization to guarantee adequate medical care for everyone. But there is a system in the sense that we have defined the term. Although no one has complete knowledge of the organization, process, and outcomes of the elements of the medical care system, we shall attempt in this chapter to outline some important known and suspected aspects.

Elements

The traditional element of the delivery of care in the U.S. is the solo private practice, operated much like a small business. The single physician sets up an office in a community of his choice, hangs out his shingle, and sells his services for a fee on a piecework basis. He makes the capital investment for the space and equipment he needs to operate his business and must make enough income to operate the practice as well as maintain himself and his family. He employs those ancillary workers he needs for the operation of the practice, maintains a method of accounting and collection of payments, maintains the supplies needed for the operation, and, in general, must have or develop enough expertise to operate a small service business. Theoretically, he is available to his patients at all times in this type of practice. He has no one with whom he can share either the business or clinical aspects of medical practice.

Solo practice remains the predominant form of health care delivery in the U.S. At least 80 percent of physicians in private practice continue to work on a solo basis. However, many if not most physicians in solo private practice have developed arrangements for coverage of their patients during nights and weekends. The solo practitioner reports in surveys that he works about 50 hours a week, 46 of these hours involving direct patient care. He works 48 weeks a year and sees an average of 126 patients a week. Most of these patients he cares for in his office; he sees an average of 28 per week in the hospital. He employs one or two allied health personnel in his practice, one of whom is often a secretary-receptionist. Nursing does not play a preeminent role in solo practice— less than one in four solo practices employ a registered nurse (AMA, 1972a).

The advantage of this form of practice, and perhaps the reason that it continues to be the dominant mode, relates to the physician's image of himself as a professional. As we discussed earlier, autonomy is an intrinsic part of the physician's socialization as a professional. In solo practice the physician at least appears almost completely autonomous. He alone decides the format, the style, and the elements of his working conditions, although substantial deviation from community expectations may result in loss of patients when there are alternatives available. Even as the corner grocery, the local cleaner, and even the solo-practice lawyer are disappearing from the American scene, a substantial number of physicians seek to remain as single entrepreneurs.

Although this form of medical practice is unlikely to disappear quickly into the fogs of history, other forms have begun to come into their own over the past several decades. Group practice has been defined as "the application of medical services by three or more physicians formally organized to provide medical care, consultation, diagnosis, and/or treatment through the joint use of equipment and personnel, and with the income from medical practice distributed in accordance with methods previously determined by members of the group" (McNamara and Todd, 1970). By this definition group practice cannot be said to be new; its origins date to the brothers Mayo in 1883 when they established what became the internationally known Mayo Clinic. The growth of group practice has been slow, but the trend toward this form of organization has increased markedly since the early 1950's. In 1900 there were only two group practices in the U.S. That number had increased to only 150 by 1930 and to 506 by 1943. By 1959 there were 1,546 groups in existence, and the rate of growth has quickened since that time. The American Medical Association reported 4,289 groups in 1965 and 6,371 by 1969. In 1969 a total of 40,093 physicians, 18 percent of all active doctors, practiced in the 6,371 medical groups. It has been suggested that, if this trend continues, group practice will be the predominant form of medical practice by the 1980's (MacLeod and Prussin, 1973).

There are three basic categories of group practice: single specialty groups, composed of physicians practicing in a single specialty; general practice groups, composed only of general practitioners or family physicians; and multispecialty groups, made up of physicians who provide care in more than one specialty. One-half of the groups reported in 1969 were of the single specialty type, while three-eighths were of the multispecialty type and the remainder of the general practice type. The average group practice contained about six physicians with multispecialty groups in general somewhat larger than the other types. Most group practices were small but a few had as many as several hundred physicians.

From the survey data accumulated by the American Medical Association, two trends seem apparent in the types of group practices being formed. Between 1965 and 1969 the previous rapid growth of single specialty groups leveled off and multispecialty groups increased as a proportion of the total. The number of general practice groups declined as a percentage of the total. This last trend is hardly surprising since the numbers of general practitioners also declined in the same period.

Group practice has become popular in particular sections of the nation. For example, three of the nine census divisions, the East North Central, the South Atlantic, and the Pacific areas, contained half of the total groups and physicians in group practice. Physicians in New England, perhaps as a vestige of their historical independence, generally do not select this format for their work. This area contained only 3.9 percent of the total number of group practices in the country.

One study noted that states that entered the union relatively late have the highest proportions of physicians in group practice while most of the original 13 colonies have the lowest proportions, suggesting that such innovations are more easily established in social systems with less firmly established traditions. Other factors related to a high proportion of physicians in group practice included low density of population, more people outside metropolitan areas, a larger proportion of young people in the population and lower per capita income (Roemer, *et al.,* 1974).

Physicians working in a group practice report working an average of 53 hours a week for 48 weeks a year, about the same as solo practitioners. During the 48 hours reportedly involved in direct patient care in a week, about 156 patients are seen, 30 more patients than physicians in solo practice report seeing during the same period. Most of these patients are seen within the confines of the physician's office, but he sees 35 percent of them in the hospital. This percentage is also somewhat higher than that for the solo practitioner.

Among other differences between the group physician and the solo practitioner is the former's greater use of allied health personnel. There are on the average 2.5 personnel per physician for all group practices compared to 1.8 per physician in solo practice (McNamara and Todd, 1970). There are few detailed studies of the productivity of physicians in any form of practice, and it is difficult to determine if group practices use this increased number of personnel to increase the productivity of the physicians of the group. We have seen that the physicians in a group tend to see more patients in the course of the work week, but it is also true that they tend to work a slightly longer week.

One other difference between the solo practitioner and the group physician worth noting is income. Average net income figures are difficult to interpret because of geographic variations in both expense and income. However, on the average the physician in a group practice has a significantly higher net income as well as a higher level of professional expense than the solo practitioner. Physicians in solo practice in 1969 made an average net income of

100

$39,138 per year with additional professional expenses averaging $20,188. In contrast, the physician in a group practice made an average of $41,376 per year in net income with professional expenses of $22,084 (AMA, 1972a).

The reasons for the increased popularity of group practice among physicians are unclear. These statistics do not indicate that the format allows the physician more leisure, nor is there any indication of a decrease in his operating expenses made possible by the pooling of resources by the members of the group. He does see more patients, perhaps as a result of the use of allied health workers. Perhaps as a result of his increased patient load, his income increases. Coverage arrangements for nights and weekends may be easier. In any event, if these statistics have any validity, the physician in group practice does have some monetary benefit from this mode of organization.

These two types of practice, solo and group, continue to be the predominant means of delivery in the U.S. medical care system, but they may be placed on a continuum of organization of the system ranging from complete autonomy for a physician in solo practice to much less autonomy of a physician in what we will call institutional practice, that is, practice in organizations with multiple levels and echelons. As we have seen, the physician in solo practice is in complete control not only of the clinical aspects of his practice but also of the managerial aspects of the service as well. In the traditional group practice, as we have described it, the physician gives up a modest amount of his autonomy in these latter aspects in order to form with his colleagues an organization that will manage the business of the group. However, the physician in the group maintains control with his colleagues over the details of the business of the organization, continues to charge patients on a piece-work basis, and decides with his peers the financial gain of the service to himself and the other members of the group. He also has complete autonomy in the clinical aspects of his work.

The physician working in an institution often does not deal with these organizational matters. In this type of practice, the details of management, finances, and policy are managed by an administration that may or may not be composed of physicians. In such an institution, the physician retains, for the most part, control over the clinical details of his work. As an employee of the institution, however, he loses in large measure the autonomy over many of the details of his daily professional life. As we shall see, this loss of autonomy over all of his professional activities has sociological implications for the profession in terms of the usual definition of "profession." Before beginning that analysis, however, we should consider some examples of institutional practice.

A growing form of institutional practice on the contemporary scene is the prepaid group practice. While not common, it is important in part because it may represent the future mode of medical care for the U.S. Probably the first prepaid group practice was formed in 1929 in Elk City, Oklahoma, by Dr. Michael Shadid as the Farmer's Union Cooperative Health Association. Since that beginning, the growth of prepaid group practice has been slow. Initially considered by the profession as a radical innovation likely to destroy the quality, quantity, and status of the profession, there has gradually been a change in attitude by the medical establishment toward prepayment. No longer are these groups condemned as the first step toward that eternal devil "socialized medicine;" indeed, in the 1970's a conservative President of the country, Richard Nixon, proposed that prepaid group practice in the form of Health Maintenance Organizations (HMO's) was to be the model of medical practice for the entire country.

While there are variations on the theme, a prepaid group practice includes several generalizable elements. The basic tenets of prepayment are seen in the Kaiser Permanente Group Plan on the West Coast of the U.S., one of the most successful of the existing prepayment group practices. First there is the element of prepayment. Each subscriber to the group pays to the program a monthly fee for membership in the program. The payment may be made by the individual, by his employer, or by some other funding agency. The medical care is delivered by a group of physicians who are paid on a capitation (per number of patients in his panel) or salaried basis by the prepayment organization rather than on a fee-for-service basis. The net income is pooled and divided on the basis of a number of equations, most of which include some incentive payment for efficiency and effectiveness. In a fee-for-service system, there is no incentive other than the physician's sense of ethics to keep costs down. If a physician owns interest in laboratories or hospitals there is the danger that these resources will be overused.

In a prepaid group practice, the patient's monthly fee usually covers such services and overuse will cost the group rather than adding to its income.

The concept of prepayment groups also includes integrated services based at or near a medical center that is equipped to manage all illnesses including hospitalization for its subscribers. Only the rare conditions are referred for care at another center, usually a university center, since the group must pay for all care of its subscribers and referral outside the system may be more expensive. The integration and coordination of facilities and services allow savings in costs, and planning of services avoids expensive duplication of procedures and facilities.

All prepaid programs pay lip service to the notion of voluntary enrollment, perhaps as a nod toward medicine's traditional aphorism that the patient should always be allowed free choice of his physician and that no one should interfere with the patient-physician relationship. Finally, the medical care in the prepaid plan is to be comprehensive in scope. The entire gamut of medical services, including hospitalization, nursing homes, and mental health care is provided, at least by some groups. Prevention and health education are considered important parts of the prepaid practice on the theory that one of the cheapest ways to provide medical care is to prevent illness (Seward, 1969).

As of 1970 the number of prepaid group practices was not large, and growth continued to be slow. In a survey done in 1965 there were 88 prepaid group practices in the U.S. in which more than half of the physician's activities involved patients who were enrolled in a prepayment plan. By 1969 there were only 85 such groups in the country (McNamara and Todd, 1970). These 85 groups contained 3,912 physicians, slightly more than 1 percent of the total number in the U.S. A few well-known group practice systems, located in California, New York, and Washington, contained 58 percent of all the physicians working in prepaid group practice. The Kaiser Permanente program, located predominantly on the West Coast and Hawaii, contains the highest number of enrollees (2.5 million) and is probably the best known of these systems. The Health Insurance Plan of Greater New York (HIP) contains 780,000 patients and is located in New York City, predominantly for city employees and their dependents.

In 1972 Congress amended the Social Security legislation so that recipients of Medicare (national health insurance for the aged) and Medicaid (medical payments to low-income families with dependent children) could receive covered services through a single capitation prepayment to a Health Maintenance Organization beginning in mid-1973. At this writing, it is too early to estimate the impact of this funding mechanism on the development of prepayment plans as a major mode of care in the medical care system of the U.S. Nevertheless, the content of the organization of these Health Maintenance Organizations resembles closely the system already described for existing prepaid group practice.

There have been some proposed modifications in the prepayment system which attempt to continue to allow the physician to collect on a fee-for-service basis with the Health Maintenance Organization continuing to collect its revenue on a capitation basis. This mixture of fee-for-service and capitation as a funding mechanism is probably a nod to the pressures from organized medicine, which has resisted prepayment plans. Other implications of this legislation for the practice of medicine and the system in which it resides will be discussed later.

While the prepaid group practice is one of the most interesting and potentially important forms of institutional practice in the U.S. at this time, there are a much larger number of physicians whose work we might characterize as institutional. For example, there are roughly 29,000 physicians engaged in teaching, research, and administration. While these physicians may not be engaged in direct patient care, many of them will continue to see patients at least sporadically. In addition, there are about 90,000 physicians whose practice is hospital-based. More than half of these are in some stage of their postgraduate training, and the remainder are staff physicians for hospitals. There are also several thousand physicians in the country who devote their professional time to public health issues not involving direct contact with patients, usually in some type of private or governmental institution.

The origin of the hospital as a place in which the sick and injured are provided medical care dates from the early Middle Ages. When Christianity became the official religion of the Roman Empire, the care of the sick and the poor became a part of the ethic of organized society. By the thirteenth century, as cities became larger, institutions were being established within the city walls, initially founded by the church and eventually taken over by municipal authorities, which were to provide medical care for the poor and the aged. Hospitals remained places primarily for the poor and infirm until the latter part of the nineteenth century. At that time the discovery of asepsis and anesthesic agents provided the impetus for a new type of institution that provided a location for surgery for all social classes. Until that time the middle and upper classes shunned hospitals as pest houses, as indeed they were, because of the lack of knowledge of the causes of infection. With the rise of these two technological advances and the concomitant development of other similar medical advances, hospitals became "temples of medicine" in which patients could usually be safely treated (Sigerist, 1960). With the technological advances, the rise in the number of hospitals and hospital beds was swift. In 1909 in the U.S. there were an estimated 4,300 hospitals with 421,000 beds; by 1928 there were about 7,000 hospitals with almost 900,000 beds (Sigerist, 1934). In 1970 there were 7,123 hospitals with 1,615,771 beds, 5,859 of which were community hospitals (AMA, 1972b).

If the scientific and technological advances have fostered the rise of the hospital as an important part of the medical care system, other developments have ensured their continued growth. Once the hospital became a safe place for treatment as well as necessary location for surgery and other techniques, the need for the funding of this care became evident. Initially, hospitals were funded as charitable institutions for the care of the poor, but the ordinary citizen, when confronted with the cost of hospitalization, often could not afford it.

The earliest company insuring against injury in the U.S. was established in 1850 in response to the demand for coverage against the frequent injuries on railroads and steamboats of the time. By the end of the Civil War, insurance companies were offering insurance for injuries of all descriptions. The first company to write a policy for general health insurance was established in 1847; in the early days the emphasis was on loss of income caused by illness. After a seven-day waiting period, the client was insured against loss of income resulting from such diseases as typhus, typhoid fever, scarlet fever, smallpox, and diphtheria. Since persons with these diseases often did not survive seven days, the plans were

105

actuarily sound if not always beneficial to the insured. The policy's duration was 26 weeks. By 1929 the pattern of medical care had changed radically and with that change, the cost of care increased, particularly the cost of hospitalization. In 1929 a group of school teachers arranged with the Baylor University Hospital in Dallas, Texas to provide them with hospital care on a prepaid basis. This move by those school teachers provided the precursor of the Blue Cross insurance concept and the development of private insurance policies against hospitalization. A further development occurred during World War II when wage increases were frozen as part of the war economy. During that period labor unions used the concept of fringe benefit as part of their collective bargaining with their employers, and one of the major fringe benefits negotiated was group health insurance (Source Book of Health Insurance Data, 1970).

After World War II, in the late 1940's, legislation was passed by the federal government to subsidize the building of hospitals within communities. This legislation resulted in the construction of or additions to large numbers of community hospitals throughout the country as a capital investment in facilities. By the early 1950's, with the formation of the National Institutes of Health, the government began to invest heavily in research in medicine. In 1947 the national expenditure for medical research was at the level of $87 million with the federal share of that figure merely $27 million. By 1966 the total figure had reached the level of $2 billion with the federal government contributing $1.4 billion. The impact of this investment in research was to increase dramatically the numbers of physicians involved in these matters, usually in hospitals, and to siphon off able physicians who would have otherwise entered other arenas of the system (Darley and Somers, 1967).

These financial subsidies of hospitals were important elements in their growth. Once the hospital could be assured of receiving its cost of operation by the mechanism of the third party, that is the insurance companies or the government, and once the patient was removed directly from the payment of the cost of hospitalization, a positive feedback system was established. The hospital could continue to expand its inpatient services as its guaranteed source of revenue. Physicians as the prime movers in the hospital were inevitably encouraged to hospitalize patients in order to protect the patient from the cost of medical care, the cost of which was spread over large groups through payment of insurance premiums. Indeed, the patient often placed pressure on the physician to hospitalize him for diagnostic evaluations which could have been done on an outpatient basis except that the cost of such evaluations would not be covered by his insurance policy. This emphasis on the inpatient aspect of the system sustained the development of the hospital industry, as well as played a role in the escalating cost of hospitalization. In short, the hospital industry, with an assured subsidy of its work, had a classic cost plus contract with the insurance industry. As the cost of hospitalization rose, the cost of insurance premiums also rose proportionally, but was spread over large numbers of people some of whom used hospitals infrequently.

The rise of hospitals as important elements of the medical care system relate to another aspect of the system which we have already discussed. The rise of the specialist physician has paralleled the rise of the hospital in the system. This physician more than the generalist needs a hospital base for a considerable proportion of his practice. Indeed, one of the sociological interpretations of the rise of modern medicine posits the hospital as one of the prime factors in its development. In the nineteenth century, with the scientific developments in such fields as bacteriology and pathology, the hospital became an important center for the congregation of patients who could serve for the study of medicine and disease. The hospital, in addition to its role in the care of the sick, continues to provide clinical laboratories for the study of disease processes (Waddington, 1973).

The increasing importance of the hospital in teaching and research in addition to patient care has resulted in a decline in what are classified as community institutions. There are several types of community hospitals according to their sponsorship. In the beginnings of the rise of hospitals in the U.S., it was common practice for an individual physician or group of physicians to sponsor and build a hospital for their own use and profit. These proprietary hospitals have decreased in number in the past 20 years; in 1970 there remained only 769 of them accounting for only 3 percent of the total number of hospital beds in the country.

As the number of proprietary hospitals has decreased, the

number of voluntary hospitals has increased. Voluntary hospitals may be defined as institutions sponsored by members of the community on a "not for profit basis." The historical development of this type of hospital began, as did many things in the U.S., with Benjamin Franklin. In the late eighteenth century Franklin and his friends established the first hospital in the U.S., the Pennsylvania Hospital, as a voluntary institution for the community. This hospital was followed shortly by the establishment of the New York Hospital, begun under a charter granted by King George III, who soon lost his creation as well as the colonies. From these early days there has been a steady evolution of these institutions; in 1970 there were 3,386 voluntary hospitals with 591,937 beds. These voluntary hospitals represent almost 70 percent of the short-term beds in the country and provide the backbone of the hospital industry.

In addition to the private sector of the hospital system, governments at various levels maintain hospital systems. There were 408 federal hospitals in 1970, largely providing medical care for servicemen and the veterans of military service. The U.S. also had 1,704 municipal hospitals in 1970, which began, and for the most part are maintained, to provide medical care for the indigent of the cities.

Finally, a significant number of hospitals (854 in 1970) have been established to provide care for patients with specific chronic diseases. There are, for example, about 100 hospitals in the U.S. that treat patients with tuberculosis.

The patterns and roles of these hospitals have changed as the modes of treatment of disease have changed with innovations in medical science. Tuberculosis is a good example of the impact of scientific innovation on the structure of the medical care system. Until the early 1950's, the treatment of tuberculosis usually included a long period of hospitalization in a sanitarium. In the 1950's, however, a specific antibiotic for the treatment of this disease became available and the need for this type of hospital decreased. In 1960 there were 238 of these sanitariums; by 1970 there were only 100 and those remaining were in the process of converting to other uses.

In contrast, while the number of chronic disease hospitals have decreased, another form of domiciliary care has evolved. The needs of the large number of elderly citizens in the population have become an increasingly important element in the medical care system. The Medicare legislation of 1965 was a response to the needs of this large population. Coincident with this legislation has been the rapid development of the nursing home as a place for the delivery of care for some of the elderly population. In 1963 there were something over 16,000 of these homes with 568,560 beds; by 1969 these had increased to more than 19,000 homes and almost one million beds (AMA, 1972b).

Organization

The location and organization of medical practice, particularly outside of institutions but often in regard to the institutions themselves, has developed in. the *laissez faire* manner of its small-business tradition. As the bulk of the population in the country has changed from a rural to a small town to an urban to a suburban mode of living, so the distribution of physicians has somewhat paralleled the movements of the population. However, there has been no mechanism to guarantee access to physicians. In 1963 there were 98 counties without a physician in the U.S. By 1970 there were 132. There was a direct correlation between the physician-patient ratio and the size of community. For example, in nonmetropolitan areas of less than 10,000 inhabitants, there was one physician for every 2,491 people; in metropolitan areas of over five million people there was one physician for every 521 people (AMA, 1972a). Not only have the rural areas become relatively deprived of physicians, but with the migration to the suburbs, the centers of metropolitan areas, which contained large numbers of indigent people, were also without primary care physicians. In the slums of major cities the medical care has been relegated to the clinics of the large hospitals still found in what at one time were prosperous areas. In the 1960's these hospitals increasingly found themselves the sole providers of medical care for a population at particular risk, at least partially because of their poverty (Kosa, *et al.,* 1969). As in any system when overloaded, the emergency and other clinics in these hospitals often were inadequate to handle the large numbers of indigent families, causing a further deterioration of their medical care.

Theoretically, the free market in medical services would result in physicians moving to areas where shortages exist in order to maximize profit where demand was greater. In reality this has not happened. While the government in the recent past, through its economic policy, has begun to influence the organization of the medical care system, the predominant influence in the system remains within the domain of the private sector. With the exceptions already noted in the form of prepaid group practice and other forms of institutional care, fee-for-service continues to be the mode of payment for physicians' services. The private citizen, from his net income, pays the physician on a piecework basis for the medical care he receives. He also pays for the laboratory and other adjunct services of the system on the same basis. With minor exceptions, until Medicare and Medicaid, insurance or other "third parties" had little influence, financial or otherwise, on medical care outside hospitals.

Theoretically, there is, in the free market system, a direct feedback loop from the client to the provider. If the patient is dissatisfied with the service he receives from the physician, he has the leverage in the form of not paying the physician's fee or changing physicians to indicate his dissatisfaction and to influence the service he receives. This formulation represents a vast oversimplification of reality. The free market works only when the market is indeed free, that is, when there is competition within the market for the delivery of the service. However, in many areas the shortage of physicians results in few if any alternatives for the person who needs medical attention. The reality is that the health market is not free, and the patient often, if not usually, does not have free choice of his physician. In addition, the client in the area of medical care is usually not competent to judge the quality of his care.

The free market analogy also presumes competition in prices of the service, but the health care service provided by physicians is not a free market in this respect either. The code of ethics of the profession states, "The prime objective of the medical profession is to render service to humanity; reward or financial gain is a subordinate consideration. . . . Poverty of a patient . . . should command the gratuitous service of the physician" (McFadden, 1967). The physician may or may not be willing or able at all times to adhere to this ideal. Most physicians are in no position to assess the financial status of the patient. Physicians in a community usually set their fees informally. Indeed the government, when financing the direct care of certain patients by means of the Medicare and Medi-

110

caid legislation, formalized this procedure by stating that the fees paid by these programs would be the "usual and customary fees" of the community. Physicians are bound by "ethics" not to advertise fees or services generally. Price competition is minimal if it occurs at all. In short, the free market analogy for pricing of services does not apply to this system.

A given physician may choose to live almost anywhere he pleases and make a more than adequate income. For whatever reason, persons who must live in places that are less desirable frequently do not have access to adequate medical care.

In our discussion of medicine as a profession we suggested that one of the major characteristics of the professional role is autonomy. Because physicians have traditionally gained that autonomy, they have had the freedom to determine their places and patterns of work and their income. But there are indications, as we have seen, that physicians are beginning to enter more organized forms of practice, which parallels similar developments in other occupations and professions, although at a slower rate in medicine. As this occurs, they must abide by rules set by the group, thereby inevitably decreasing some of their individual freedom.

One issue that has fascinated some sociologists is the comparison of organizations that provide professional services to clients and organizations that manufacture products or provide other services (Blau and Scott, 1962). All formal organizations have rules that allocate specific tasks to specific individuals, called the division of labor. In few organizations can a single individual perform every task in the process of making the product or providing the service. Usually, a product can be made more rapidly and cheaply if the tasks involved in its production are simplified and each are assigned to an individual on some sort of assembly line. By calculating the time needed to do each task, managers can assign specific numbers of people to specific tasks and the assembly line flows more or less smoothly. Groups of individuals performing a set of tasks are assigned a supervisor, who acts as a watchdog over the quantity and quality of work, reallocates people and technology as breakdowns and other contingencies arise, and coordinates the work of the group with supervisors of other groups. The number of people in the organization and the complexity of technology and tasks has an effect on the number of people per supervisor (Haire, 1959). Usually supervisors have supervisors in a pyramidal hierarchy of management.

The term bureaucracy was assigned to such organizations by an early analyst (Weber, 1947 edition), who emphasized the rationality and efficiency of the system. The word bureaucracy has acquired, in its popular connotation, a pejorative meaning, eliciting visions of mountains of "red tape," inefficiency, and mindless routine. While popular meanings of words do not necessarily reflect accurately the circumstances they describe, there is little question that some bureaucracies fit the popular image. Informal norms for productivity develop that are not necessarily congruent with the formal norms of the organization and which may be enforced by peers with more vigor than are formal norms by supervisors (Roy, 1952). New norms may be negotiated and formalized in union contracts. Problems in coordination of activities occur because of breakdowns in communication channels, many similar to those described in our discussion of the physician-patient relationship. Chains of authority may not always be clear. For example, the maintenance or housekeeping supervisor may not agree with the production supervisor as to the proper task of a worker at a given time, and the worker is given conflicting orders.

An overall survey of medical service organizations has not been done with respect to each of these characteristics. Clearly some medical service organizations, particularly large hospitals, have some of the characteristics of bureaucratic organizations, sometimes with attendant efficiencies and sometimes with attendant problems (Perrow, 1965).

Process

One inventory of generalizations about the effectiveness of organization (defined as degree of goal-achievement) exempted professional organizations from many (Price, 1968). Because of the complexity of the knowledge involved in medical diagnosis and treatment, and its almost exclusive control by the physician, the major tasks of diagnosis and prescription of treatment have not been divided into simple tasks assigned to different people. Some attempts at history-taking and diagnosis by allied personnel or computers are under way, but it is doubtful that decisions of these personnel or computers will be accepted without review by a physician, at least in the near future.

Nurse associates and physicians' assistants (persons not trained in nursing but more on the model of military corpsmen) are being trained in some areas to take histories and provide some routine treatment. Their work is reviewed by a physician who usually makes the final decision. These modes of medical care have not been evaluated well enough to draw conclusions regarding their effectiveness. The decrease in contact between physician and patient could result in loss of the advantages of such continuity, noted earlier. In emergency care where continuity is not at issue, such as among ambulance crews, training like that of corpsmen is particularly desirable.

Where the technology is highly developed and tasks can be divided somewhat, as in surgery or radiology, the process does resemble an assembly line. But the major decisions are made by the physicians. The more sophisticated hospitals have committees of professionals that review autopsies and other pathological reports with the inherent threat of disciplinary action, but the discipline seldom goes beyond the reminder that a mistake was made. In most medical service organizations physicians have no professional supervisors (Bucher, 1970).

The conflict between a bureaucracy and a profession is seen most clearly in a hospital. Most voluntary hospitals are overseen by a board of directors consisting of a group of citizens, often wealthy and influential, who serve as an act of *noblesse oblige* to the community. The hospital is administered by a group of managers who must answer to this board of directors. These administrators may be laymen or physicians but, whatever their background, their concern is with the efficient running of the hospital.

The field of hospital administration is a comparatively new occupation in the medical care system and attracts young people who view the hospital in the same ways that a young graduate of the Harvard Business School views General Motors. The work of the hospital is executed by physicians whose training and concern lies not in issues of efficiency and business management but in the medical care of patients. This "company of equals" often does not adhere to or even acknowledge the rules of the administration.

113

When there is a conflict in the priorities of the institution for space, capital investment, or manpower, the administration of the hospital, if it is not able to convince the physicians of the need and value of the decisions made, may find themselves victims of not so subtle blackmail. The physicians may threaten overtly to go directly to the board of directors, whose members are more likely to be impressed with the expert knowledge of the physicians (Perrow, 1965).

In larger hospitals there is likely to be a group of physicians whose role it is to bridge the gap between the profession and the administration. Each specialty in the hospital will have a chief of its service, who has an allegiance to both the administration of the entire hospital as well as to his individual service. They are acknowledged by the other physicians in the service to have the authority to decide the working hours of the physicians, the amount of space allowed each physician, and, in the case of salaried physicians, the level of salary for each physician within stated guidelines. While each of these chiefs has this administrative authority, his power over the clinical practice of medicine is much less direct and much more subtle. In issues of control of patient care, the chief of the service can only suggest or consult with the individual physician about the care of the latter's patient. In short, the control of the clinical practice of the physician within a hospital, as elsewhere, is by his peers in the form of informal and often symbolic sanctions (Goss, 1961; Susser and Watson, 1971).

The administration in the hospital is left free to manage many aspects of the institution, as long as they do not impinge on the autonomy of the physician. Such matters as financing, management of ancillary personnel, and bookkeeping are all left to the administration as long as the individual physician is not affected. Any one of these matters may become a battleground for a conflict between the bureaucrat and the professional if the physician perceives his autonomy or status threatened. Even in the most advanced and successfully managed hospitals, these issues are not completely and successfully resolved at all times.

The relationships among professionals in hospitals also present problems. Contrary to the television image of the nurse-physician relationship, one study of a large teaching hospital found little face-to-face communication. Physicians' instructions to nurses were often written, and if nurses had useful information about patients, it was seldom communicated to physicians (Duff and Hollingshead, 1968).

Nurses in hospitals have made the transition from a more professional role to a more bureaucratic one. These traditional members of the health team who work in hospitals have, in large measure, given up the direct care of patients for the management of the hospital ward or floor. As part professional and part administrator, they often find themselves standing between the physician interested in the care of his patient and the administration interested in the care of the organization. This delicate balance gives the nurse an especially potent, if hazardous, role in the hospital (Abdellah, 1954; Lambertson, 1967).

One other aspect of the nursing role within the hospital gives nurses power. With the exception of residents and interns, and also of a few full-time physicians (in less than 10 percent of general hospitals), physicians do not practice full-time in hospitals (Roemer and Friedman, 1971). Indeed, most spend a minority of their practice seeing patients in hospitals. Nurses usually are the single individuals with professional training who do spend all of their working day within hospitals and for that reason provide the element of continuity for the management of other workers. This continuity allows the nurse to wield more power than her role indicates. She manages the execution of this power by avoiding confrontation with the physician, while in fact carrying out and often deciding the management of the hospital ward.

There is pressure within the nursing profession to return to the direct care of patients in an expanded and more autonomous role. If large numbers of nurses select this role model, then the management of the day-to-day activities of the hospital must be assumed by others. It is unclear if these trends will be sustained. However, in larger hospitals, ward managers, lay persons with no clinical training, are being used to assume the management of the non clinical matters on the individual hospital ward or floor.

The bureaucratic organization of a hospital impinges more on interns and residents than on other physicians. Young physicians, upon completion of their medical school education, enter a period of postgraduate education, the residency, during which time they are based in a hospital, often a university medical center. This training program is arranged in a two or three level heirarchy of interns and junior and senior residents. Until the mid-1960's, the residency was considered an exclusively education process and, therefore, one in which the young physician in the interests of his education was expected to commit himself exclusively to that end. The hours were long, the salaries low or nonexistent, and the living conditions difficult. This pattern of postgraduate education had existed for at least 30 years in the U.S., since the development of specialty training. Little or no recognition was given to the fact that many hospitals depended upon interns and residents for essential services.

In the mid-1960's, however, the young house officers, as the residents are called, recognized this fact and began to organize as a group. The need for such trainees to carry on the work of the hospital had expanded, and the length of the training period changed radically. Within four or five years, the salaries of the house officers increased by several hundred percent throughout the country, and their working conditions improved measurably. The physician who previously had worked 48 hours at a time began to demand and get eight-hour working days with night-on-call rotation of every third night.

Doubtless many factors explain this phenomenon, not the least of which are the ordinary laws of the market, supply and demand, but a change in the young physician's vision of himself seems also a reasonable possibility. The resident physician may see himself more an employee of an institution, the hospital, than as a professional using the facilities of the hospital for his education and the care of his patients. When the physician begins to lose his identity as the professional with a primary commitment to his patient, he is freed to begin with little impunity to negotiate with the bureaucracy on more mundane issues. That is, the professional, in this instance the resident, demands of the organization a set of rules and regulations that define in clearer terms his responsibility to the organization. This represents a shift from the traditional image of the physician who sacrifices his own gratifications in his patients' interests. Obviously, because he is negotiating with the institution as part of a group, an individual must give up some of his autonomy.

There is other evidence within the profession of similar activity. Unions of physicians have until recently been anathema to the profession, and certainly unionized physicians indulging in strike activity was once unthinkable. Yet in the past ten years we have seen one physicians' strike in Canada (Badgely and Wolfe, 1967), as well as strikes in metropolitan areas of groups of physicians employed by governmental agencies.

Of course, the American Medical Association for several generations acted as the spokesman for the individual physician in government circles as well as to the general public. It can be argued that this organization is but a union in businessmen's clothing. Nevertheless, whether we are talking about the AMA or about one of the new unions, the individual physician who belongs to one relates to a group which, through its bureaucracy, determines many of the external details of his work. This is a far cry from the position of the solo practitioner who determines much of the details of his everyday professional life without reference to outside forces.

Once the organization defines the details of his work for the professional, there arises the possibility that the latter may change his basic attitude toward that work (Roy, 1952). If the organization defines the minimum work expected of the physician and the physician's allegiance turns toward the organization rather than to himself or to the profession, then his stake in his work may change and the work may become a job rather than a profession. There is some empirical evidence of differences in productivity of salaried and fee-for-service physicians. The physician on salary sees fewer patients and works fewer hours than his colleague who is working more autonomously on a fee-for-service basis (AMA, 1972a). While the data are difficult to interpret, since the physician on a salary may be doing other tasks in addition to his direct patient care and the fee-for-service physician may work more simply to make more money, it is interesting that these differences exist.

The physician in a salaried position within an organization may find himself in a conflict-of-interest situation if the interest of his patient and the interest of the organization are not congruent. Studies of physicians in the armed forces have shown that such conflicts are not uncommon in this setting and that when they arise they are likely to be settled in the interest of the organization rather than that of the patient (Daniels, 1972). The physician who elects to place his professional judgment in support of his patient against the interests of the organization may find himself relieved of duty or otherwise punished. Such an episode occurred in the case of a physician in Vietnam who found himself courtmartialed and sent to jail for not obeying orders.

Other aspects of large-scale organizations can be found in the bureaucratic organizations of professionals. As we have seen, the basic process of the practice of medicine resides in the physician-patient relationship. If the physician begins to relate primarily to the organization, then his relationship with his patient may become depersonalized. The advantage of the corner grocery store was its personal service and relationship with the grocer. The disadvantage of the chain grocery store is its depersonalized approach to selling food. Customers tolerate this disadvantage for the tradeoff of increased savings and convenience. Patients, who are generally in a state of anxiety, may find the supermarket approach to the practice of medicine more difficult to accept. There is some evidence that this situation has already developed in the large medical centers. The earlier mentioned study of interns in community and university hospitals showed that the intern in the university hospital, a more definite bureaucracy, often related more to the rules of the organization than to the needs of the patients (Mumford, 1970). Whether the advantages of the efficiency of a well-run bureaucracy and the personal touches of a cottage industry can be combined to capture the best of all possible worlds remains to be seen. The samples of other segments of the service industries, airlines, groceries, automobile repair, do not encourage a sanguine outlook.

The patient entering the hospital is forced to relinquish many of his usual human rights and privileges, and is expected to adhere to the system's discipline, foreign to him (Duff and Hollingshead, 1968). One of the difficult problems facing contemporary society is that of trying to make human service systems more efficient while at the same time making them responsive to human needs. In no area of our everyday life is this issue thrown in sharper focus than in the modern hospital.

Outcome

The areas of hospitals, private, semiprivate, and wards, have reflected the social class divisions of society, as have the distributions of physicians in the community. In one study, senior physicians and private duty nurses were seen often on the floors where private rooms were located, less so in semiprivate areas, and infrequently on wards. Medical and nursing students were more frequently seen on the wards serving patients of lower socioeconomic status. The consequences of medical care organization and processes are difficult to assess because the medical problems among social classes in different areas of the hospital, or in particular types of clinics and practices, are often not comparable (Duff and Hollingshead, 1968). There is some evidence, however, that the type of expertise available, the organization of care, and the treatment prescribed produces differential results in mortality, disability, and morbidity. Without question there are differences in comfort, satisfaction, and cost.

Medical care for the upper and middle classes has been delivered largely by the private system in the form of solo or group practice on a fee-for-service basis with very little of the bureaucratic problems we have noted. Medical care for the poor, on the other hand, has within the past 50 years become the responsibility of government and has become enmeshed in welfare and hospital bureaucracies. Perhaps because the entire system has not been organized rationally and because there are several systems providing parallel services, the care of the poor has suffered in its humane and technical quality.

Public health clinics run by the city or county public health establishments, municipal hospitals run by local government, university hospitals anxious for patients for teaching purposes, all, traditionally have provided medical care for low-income families. Since there has been little integration of these services, the care of the poor can be characterized as episodic, impersonal, and crisis-oriented. While the middle-class patient can choose his physician, at least where more than one are available, and has the opportunity to establish some rapport with him, the welfare patient has little choice in medical services and little opportunity to establish a relationship with any physician or health professional.

The results of differences in the systems of care are seen in such indices as infant mortality rates calculated by race. For example, the infant mortality rate (deaths per 1,000 children in the first year of life) in 1970 for white infants was 17.4 per 1,000 live births, while the rate for black infants was 31.4 per 1,000 live births. We do not mean to imply that all black citizens are of the lower socioeconomic status, but certainly this segment of our population is overrepresented in the lower social classes. The infant mortality rate is but a crude measure of the effectiveness of a health system, since the death of infants is a multifactorial phenomenon that includes such other environmental factors as housing, income, nutrition, and education. Nevertheless, such indices as these can be used to infer that differences in the health care system for the social classes account for at least some of the difference in outcomes (AMA, 1972b).

The system of care for the poor contains all of the invidious characteristics of a bureaucracy with little of its advantages. The care is provided by personnel with little stake in its quality, great difficulty in bridging the social-class barriers, and little integration of services. In 1965 Congress passed the Medicare-Medicaid legislation which provided financial subsidy for the care of the elderly and a federal financial subsidy for health care for poor families with children. This legislation has proven that the mere input of money to the system does not inevitably improve it. The principle that tinkering with a small part of a system as complex as that of medical delivery for low-income people does not alter the output has been documented amply by this natural experiment (Stevens and Stevens, 1970).

As part of the "War on Poverty," other experiments in the delivery of medical care for low-income groups were begun in the mid-1960's. The Office of Economic Opportunity established a number of so-called comprehensive care clinics in the neighborhoods of low-income families. The programs were designed essentially to mimic the idealized version of the middle-class delivery system, with one physician whose responsibility it was to relate to the patient, with heavy emphasis on preventive measures of health, and with active measures to reach out to the population in casefinding and in marketing of the service. We will take up the results of these care programs in more detail when we discuss the community factors in medical care. There is some empirical evidence of some results of these systems. For example the infant mortality rates have been reported to have decreased with the introduction of comprehensive neighborhood programs in certain areas of Denver (Chabot, 1971).

The results of longer-term advances in the medical care system are evident in the population at large. In 1940 the infant mortality rate was 47.0 per thousand; in 1970 this rate had decreased to 19.8 per thousand. In 1940 the maternal mortality rate per 100,000 live births was at a level of 376.0, while in 1970 this rate had decreased to 27.4. While some unknown proportion of these changes resulted from other factors such as better nutrition, perhaps most of the credit must go to the medical care system. The lowered infant death rate contributed substantially to the average length of life, which increased from 47.3 years in 1900 to 70.8 years in 1970 (AMA, 1972b).

Measurement of the outcome of the medical care system at this time must concern itself with additional measures of success or failure. Several have been proposed. Perhaps the most common typology of measures in current use has the poetic advantage of alliteration: death, disease, disability, discomfort, and dissatisfaction. While these words have some meaning, it rapidly becomes obvious to researchers in the field that the measurement of these outcomes is complicated, for the question must be asked, as compared to what? Another set of outcome variables has been proposed that is somewhat more specific. These seven categories include longevity, activity, disease, comfort, satisfaction, achievement, and resilience. Each of these categories implies a continuum of extremes: alive to dead (exact point of death is not always clear), functional to disabled, without detectable disease to asymptomatic disease to symptomatic disease, achieving to not achieving, and resistant to vulnerable (Starfield, 1973).

Having indicated some possible measures of outcome in the study of the medical care system, we must at this point note that the research in the field is at best fragmentary. Few studies of any medical care system have measured the outcome of its programs in terms of the outputs mentioned above. More seriously, while a few studies have examined a few of the inputs, the process, or the outcomes of a medical care system, correlations among these factors usually have not been done. We will not completely understand the medical care system until the correlations among these dimensions are studied.

The input that has received the most attention in recent years is money. In the years between 1950 and 1971 the total expenditure for health care in the U.S. rose from $12.1 billion in 1949–50 to $75 billion in 1970–71. In terms of percent of the gross national product, 4.6 percent was expended in 1949–50 and 7.4

percent in 1970–71 (Rice and Cooper, 1972). The Consumer Price Index, used to measure the price of goods and services purchased by urban wage earners and clerical workers, includes a component for health care. This index clearly shows the magnitude of the price inflation in the health care system for the consumer. In the five-year period, 1966–71, the overall consumer price index increased by 38 percent. The price index for physicians' services increased by 39 percent, and the index indicated a remarkable increase of 91.4 percent for hospital daily service charges. In perhaps more meaningful terms, the average expense per patient day in a community hospital in 1950 was $15.62; by 1970 this charge had risen to $81.01.

The reasons for this escalation of the cost to the consumer of medical care is multifold, but at its basis lies the old and venerable law of supply and demand. In the decades since the end of World War II, the U.S. has enjoyed a period of relative affluence and prosperity. The birth rate rose until recently, and the total numbers of the population increased. In addition, the numbers of the population with higher income and education also rose over this time. Increasing sophistication and education along with a rising standard of living have brought about a considerable increase both in the demand for medical care and in the utilization of the medical care system. When demand overruns the supply of goods and/or services in an uncontrolled market, the price tends to increase sharply. The demand for medical services increased sharply while the supply has been more controlled and thus the price has quickly increased.

The problem is not simply one of supply and demand. Also affecting costs are the changes in the technology and skills needed to care for patients. This increase in technology is seen particularly in regard to the hospitalized patient. The supply and maintenance of this technology is inevitably more expensive. In 1925 a patient admitted to a hospital with suspected pneumonia, given the available technology, was given, at most, nursing care and perhaps an x ray. In the 1970's, a patient with suspected pneumonia receives much more of the technical apparatus of the hospital. He may get estimations of the level of oxygen in his blood or elaborate biochemical studies of the homeostatic mechanisms of his body. All such advances in the ability of medicine to diagnose and treat patients have increased the cost and the price of care.

We might add parenthetically that, to the degree that the medical care system has prolonged life, it has had other economic consequences. Most of the population survives to the age in which the degenerative and chronic diseases are prevalent. This prolongation of life, in addition to its social consequences, involves relatively large amounts of medical care for chronic conditions. There is increasing demand for medical care for the elderly with chronic diseases, raising both the cost and price of the services. In 1970 the per capita annual expenditure for all medical care for those under 19 years was about $123, for those 19 to 64 years it was $300 dollars, and for the age group over 65 years, $790 (Cooper and McGee, 1971).

Also partially accounting for the cost of hospital care is the increase in both the numbers and salaries of the personnel working in hospitals. Traditionally, the wages of hospital workers below the professional level have been among the lowest in the American work force. In 1950, for example, the average annual hospital salary was $1,817 compared to $3,033 for an average annual wage in manufacturing. By 1967, the average hospital wage was at a level of $4,476 compared to $5,975 for a worker in manufacturing. In addition to the wage increases for nonprofessional workers, salaries for interns and residents working in the larger hospitals have also increased dramatically. Traditionally these physicians in training were paid, at best, subsistence wages in return for the opportunity for training. By the late 1960's, however, they had begun to demand and to receive salaries in the range of $12,000–$15,000 a year (AMA, 1972b).

The price of medical care for the elderly and dependent children, who often could not afford insurance, was temporarily ameliorated by the Medicare-Medicaid legislation of 1965. By the 1970's national health insurance was being debated in congress. Recognition of issues other than cost are becoming evident in some of the debates. Thus the price issue is forcing a new look by the community and society at overall planning for the organization, process, and, to some degree, control of the medical care system.

7
Health and medical care at the community level

Perhaps to most people the major resources perceived as protecting health are physicians and hospitals. The television heroes, Marcus Welby in the community and Ben Casey in the hospital, are symbols of the two extremes of medical practice, the all-wise general practitioner and the highly trained specialist. But the physician usually sees an individual after he has been injured or becomes ill. With the exception of immunizations and advice, physicians, as individuals, have little control over the forces that contribute to illness and injury and that provide access to treatment. These forces range from the contents of drinking water to the treatment and disposal of sewage, from zoning ordinances regulating the location of hospitals and physicians' offices to the decisions regarding protection from injury in vehicles used for travel.

The decisions controlling these forces usually are not made by a single individual but result from governmental or private organizational policies. In some instances no decisions or poor decisions are reached because no individual or organization has a clear responsibility and accountability for them. In other instances the systems involved may be in competition or conflict over the proper course of action. The level of the social order at which decisions and actions should be taken is often undecided as well. Constitutions, laws, or executive fiat may prescribe that decisions be made at levels far removed from the individuals or from organizations that are in a position to implement them.

In this and the next two chapters we shall discuss social organization and processes at the community, societal, and intersocietal levels that affect the health of people and the management of illness and trauma. Research on these organizations and processes is even more difficult and less frequently done than the study of individual health and illness behavior and the organization of medical care. However, as we shall see from a selected review of what is available, its importance cannot be underrated.

Informal Organization

As in most human endeavor, much of the behavior of individuals in communities is regulated by informal sanctions: frowns and smiles, gossip and compliments, blame and praise. The informal organization of the community is difficult to trace in precise and accurate terms. However, with imaginative research methods, one can define the informal organization of community groups and measure some of the output of such informal organizational systems.

One of the best studies of this genre showed that informal organizations of physicians in four communities affected individuals' tendencies to prescribe a new drug (Coleman, Katz and Menzel, 1966). Among the study's merits was the fact that the researchers did not depend exclusively on the people involved, the physicians, to report in a survey when and for what reason they prescribed the new drug. Instead, pharmacy records were checked for a three-day sampling period each month for a number of months after the drug became available. The pattern of use of the drug was correlated with the informal relationships among physicians and other factors, including information obtained by questionnaires. Using questions aimed at assessing whom among his colleagues a physician considered as "friends," "discussion partners," and/or "advisors," the researchers reconstructed the informal networks of relationships. Physicians highly integrated in these informal systems prescribed the drug earlier than their more isolated colleagues. Other factors such as formal affiliations in hospitals and partnerships were also related to use of the drug but not as strongly as position in the informal systems.

The formalization of decision-making regarding drug prescription as well as other medical procedures has occurred to some degree in some hospitals through such techniques as formalized consultations, and formal review of hospital records. And, as we shall see later, there is some movement toward auditing the records of individual practitioners in the community. The process and outcome of such a formal system of review is an interesting and important subject that deserves intensive research.

To formalize completely the decision-making process would be at the minimum cumbersome. It is questionable that it would always be in the patient's best interest. A number of forces resist such formalization, not the least of which is the resistance of physicians to any encroachment on their traditional autonomy. Also, processes once formalized are often difficult to change, although this difficulty may be less than that required to change many informal processes.

Often a mixture of formal and informal norms arises in response to rapid changes in or among systems. This is particularly true when technology changes rapidly and the formal norms develop more slowly. For example, the rapid increase in the frequency and variety of complex surgical procedures has occurred without an accompanying change in the systems that collect and dispense the large amounts of blood needed for patients undergoing some of these surgical procedures. As many as 60 pints of blood can be used in one case of open-heart surgery. Yet the United States entered the 1970's with "no national or even state blood program, and no single or responsible authority at federal or state level" (Titmuss, 1971).

Blood banks are operated by private organizations such as the Red Cross (which is dependent on charity for funds), hospitals, and profit-making commercial sources. There is little informal and less formal coordination among the blood bank systems within or between communities, often resulting in a shortage in one area and a surplus in another. Since blood cannot be stored indefinitely, some waste occurs despite an overall short supply. To increase the blood supply, a variety of systems, formal and informal, have developed in the organizations involved. In some hospitals patients are expected to replace, at future dates, the blood they use on a given occasion, sometimes two to three times more than they used. Inducements to donate blood are offered in some labor unions and business organizations in such forms as holidays and tickets to sports events. "Captive volunteers" in prisons and the armed forces may receive certain privileges or favorable treatment for giving blood. And some organizations simply buy blood, often from people in skid row areas. Many of these donors have hepatitis, malaria, or syphilis, all of which can be transmitted to the recipients of the transfusions (Titmuss, 1971).

Governmental Organization

Various levels of governmental organization have the authority to finance and regulate many of the factors affecting health. However, the exercise of government authority does not operate independently of the ideologies and private organizations in the community or society to be governed. One textbook on community health states: "In a democracy the individual is responsible for his own health. Yet a democracy recognizes there are some things important in the promotion of health that the individual cannot do for himself and the government must do for him. There are also some things that the individual can do for himself but that can be done better on a community or cooperative basis" (Anderson, 1969). This statement reflects the peculiar American ideology that confuses democracy with individualism and accepts collective action by individuals to accomplish desirable ends, at least through government action, as only a last resort. In point of fact the right of individuals to elect a representative government, the essence of democracy, has nothing to do with the individual's responsibility for his health.

This strong emphasis on individual freedom and responsibility in American ideology is coupled with a strong belief that there is a unique American social system, "the American way of life" (Arieli, 1964). Informal and, occasionally, formal sanctions are imposed on nonconformists whose hair, dress, or style of life does not comply with the majority view. The historical origins of this paradoxical mix of the insistence that the United States is a land of individual liberty and the demand for adherence to a strong set of social norms as to how one should live are beyond the scope of this work. Their existence, however, must be recognized to understand the governmental organization (or the lack thereof in some cases) as a factor in community actions regarding health.

The founders of the government of the United States wrote a document, The Constitution, that is a government limiting document. Certain individual rights, such as freedom of speech, were not supposed to be abridged by any government but considerable leeway was left to particular levels of government to promote the welfare of all people. Certain powers are defined appropriate for the federal government and other powers are left to the states. State constitutions in turn define certain powers as appropriate to state government and leave remaining powers to local communities. To some, limitation of government is deemed more important than governmental action to solve problems.

The Local Government Level

Figure 7-1. Typical Formal Organizational Structure of Local Government in the United States

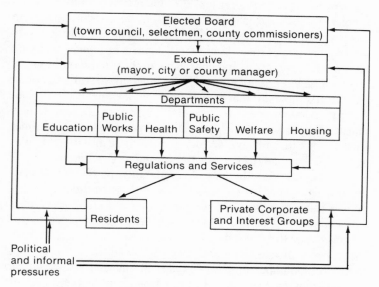

Figure 7–1 presents an outline of the organization of local community government in the United States. Such general policies as the types of programs to be undertaken, their budgets, and the

sources and amounts of taxes to implement them are decided by a group of elected officials such as the councilmen, selectmen, or county commissioners. An executive, such as a mayor or city manager, either elected or appointed, must implement the programs and collect the taxes. Executive activities of the government are usually carried out in various departments whose size and number depend upon the number and complexity of the programs undertaken by the government. These programs involve both services and the enforcement of regulations.

The citizens of the community theoretically control the government through the feedback mechanism of the ballot. Decisions about particular programs may be made by popular referendum, but many are made by elected officials, often on the advice of the executive who receives recommendations from his various executive departments.

Private corporations and interest groups, external to the formal organization of government, usually have more influence on the government than unorganized ordinary residents of the community. By the very fact of their organization, these groups can create pressures on various levels of government to implement programs and policies that are of special benefit or interest to them. At times these programs and policies are in the interest of the entire community, but it is not unusual for such groups to seek and obtain policies and programs that are detrimental to segments of the community or to the whole community. These special interests may marshal their influence for personal or corporate gain, but at times their actions are based on ideological grounds or misinformation as to what policies are in their or the community's interest.

Sociological theories of community power are diverse. Some have argued that communities tend to be controlled, usually behind the scenes, by a "power elite," a small group of families whose ownership of the major wealth gives them predominant influence over the major decisions in the community. Others have hypothesized that community power is "pluralistic," that is, that there are a number of power groups in the community whose interests may or may not converge, depending on the prevalent issues at the time (Hawley and Wirt, 1968). Studies of smaller communities tend to support the pluralistic theories (Lowry, 1962; Wildavsky, 1964; Schaffer and Schaffer, 1970). Since larger communities tend to be even more diverse, most communities, with the possible exception of those with only one industry, have multiple centers of economic and political power.

Unless an industry is involved in issues of pollution or taxes to support community health programs, it is unlikely that these power centers present a solidified coalition on health-related issues. Occasionally health issues come to the attention of a community because of the special interest or bias of a citizen or community leader. However, because of the expertise needed to understand health matters, they are usually left to trained personnel in the health and other departments of government (Conant, 1968).

Almost all county governments have a health department as do many larger municipalities. The services and regulatory authority of these health departments vary considerably from one to another. Subsections of these departments usually include:
(1) vital statistics, (2) communicable disease control, (3) maternal and infant health, (4) child health, (5) adult health, (6) mental health, (7) environmental health, (8) laboratory service, and (9) health education.
The names of these sections do not imply complete regulation or services in a given area.

The local health department is mainly responsible for implementing health codes and regulations. It does not compete with private physicians in areas such as maternal and infant health, child health, and adult health. For example, health departments operate so-called "well-baby clinics" to provide checkups and immunizations to children whose families cannot afford private services. A child with illness symptoms brought to a well-baby clinic is not examined and treated but is sent to a private physician or hospital clinic. However, until recently, public health facilities accounted for only about 1 percent of visits to physicians (Stoeckle, 1969).

A few health departments, hospitals, universities, and community-organized corporations have opened neighborhood health centers for low-income families as part of the federal antipoverty programs initiated during the 1960's. The goal of these programs was to provide comprehensive care to patients whose medical treatment previously had been fragmented among well-baby clinics, hospital emergency and outpatient specialty clinics, and, occasionally, private physicians (Parks, 1968). One study in Boston found

131

that families bringing a child to a hospital emergency clinic had used an average of nearly four separate pediatric facilities in the preceding year (Robertson, *et al.,* 1974). The future of these neighborhood health centers for the poor is problematic and depends on their ability to develop and maintain a reliable base of financial support to survive in the face of loss of funds that might occur during the tenure of conservative governmental administrations.

To a degree some of the neighborhood health centers increased the individual citizens roles in decision-making. The Economic Opportunity Act of 1964 called for "maximum feasible participation" of the poor in the control of the authorized antipoverty programs. As a result, many of the boards of directors of neighborhood health centers were elected from the community to be served, rather than being appointed from among prominent citizens as was the case for health advisory committees of traditional health departments and other health organizations. Although participation in these elections was often low and elected directors not always representative of the community, new channels of communication between health professionals and their clientele were opened. The development of knowledge and leadership skills among persons not accustomed to medical jargon and organizational procedures was often difficult. Angry confrontations and some inefficiency resulted inevitably. But health professionals and patients learned from one another and, perhaps, had an impact on the health problems of the community (Hallman, 1970).

The activities of other departments of community government often have as much impact on health matters as those of the health department itself. But the activities of these various departments often are un-coordinated (Anderson, 1969). Such departments as the Department of Public Works, Public Housing Authority, Department of Welfare, and Department of Hospitals (where separated from the Department of Health), have direct responsibility for a number of services and regulations related to health matters. Departments responsible for schools, police, fire protection, and agricultural agencies also conduct health-related activities. In addition to the programs of these governmental departments, nongovernmental groups such as civic clubs, church groups, parent-teacher associations, the Red Cross, and the March of Dimes often launch special programs directed toward special health-related problems. These programs may be coordinated or they may overlap or work at cross-purposes. Private health-related enterprises such as proprietary hospitals, private physicians, and nursing homes may or may not cooperate with the government programs depending both on ideological notions as to what should be private and what should be public activity, and on their perception of the degree to which government programs are competing with their own self-interest and prerogatives.

Community Decision Processes

Sometimes because of and sometimes despite these programs, the general health of people in most communities in the U.S. has improved over time. Such measures as purification of water, the pasteurization of milk, and sewage disposal have been accepted, though not always easily, as appropriate community concerns and have resulted in dramatic reductions in disease rates. Other policies such as the fluoridation of water to lower tooth decay rates have not yet been accepted in many communities. The fluoridation controversy provides a good illustration of the roles various groups play in a community decision on a controversial health matter.

Any of the mentioned governmental or private groups can initiate a proposal to improve the public's health. In the case of fluoridation of water, dentists were the initial enthusiastic supporters of the proposal. Following the discovery that children in communities with natural fluorine in water supplies had considerably lower rates of tooth decay than those in communities without fluorine, field studies were developed in a few communities to test the effect on tooth decay as well as its possible side effects (McNeil, 1957). Already convinced that fluorine was effective and unwilling to wait for the results of the field studies, a group of dentists in Wisconsin began a campaign for the fluoridation of water supplies in the state.

Opposition to fluoridation developed in a variety of groups. Some opponents questioned the wholesale adoption of fluoridation until the evidence that it was not harmful could be obtained, while others opposed it on the basis of cost to taxpayers or the ideological principle of limiting governmental interference in matters that people could care for themselves. Even after the U.S. Public Health Service and the American Dental Association began to advocate fluoridation on the basis of the preliminary results of the field studies, the controversy continued in many communities.

133

The fluoridation controversy was somewhat unique among public health decisions. Many local communities decided the issue by referendum rather than by the more usual process of decisions by authorities (Sapolsky, 1968; Crain *et al.,* 1969). The precedent was set in Stevens Point, Wisconsin, a town that gained considerable notoriety as a result of the fight over fluoridation. When fluoridation was first proposed by the local dental society and board of health, a local self-appointed government watchdog raised opposition and, when he was joined by others, the city council defeated the proposal. Advocates of fluoridation then elicited the support of many women's clubs in the community. After being presented with a 37-foot-long petition, the city council reversed its decision. The opposition then marshaled its forces and obtained enough signatures to force a referendum on the matter under Wisconsin law. Meanwhile, equipment had been purchased and the water fluoridated. Opponents charged that this was done in secret and that "officials had tried to fool the public" (McNeil, 1957). Both sides contacted "experts" in universities in the state and elsewhere, who gave often cautious or conflicting opinions. The battle raged in letters-to-the-editor with name-calling, claims that the water tasted bad (even during the period when there was no fluorine in the water), and concerns that fluorine was poisonous (it is in sufficient concentration as is chlorine, used to purify many water supplies; neither is toxic to human beings at the concentrations used in water supplies). The battle became so bitter that many local dentists who might have influenced the decision withdrew from the fight. The fluoridation proposal was defeated by referendum (McNeil, 1957).

The history of the fluoridation controversy in Stevens Point illustrates a number of known principles that operate during community conflict. Members of communities tend to cluster into opposing groups depending on their previous positions on other issues. Old fights among the opponents tend to color their pronouncements and actions on the issue at hand; the controversy becomes personalized rather than being based on the substantive issue. Coleman (1957) has proposed a "Gresham's law of conflict":

The harmful and dangerous elements drive out those which would keep the conflict in bounds. Reckless, unrestrained leaders head the attack; combat organizations arise to replace the mild and more constrained preexisting organizations; derogatory and scurrilous charges replace dispassionate issues; antagonism replaces disagreement, and a drive to ruin the opponent takes the place of the initial will to win.

The fact that fluoridation referenda are more often defeated when there is a larger turnout of voters in the community has been attributed, in part, to these phenomena. When issues are not controversial, voter turnout tends to be low and consists mainly of members of the middle and upper classes who have been taught it is their duty to vote or who do so because they have the greatest economic and social stake in the community. When issues become controversial, the citizens less attached to various community organizations and groups are more likely to become involved in the conflict and to vote, if only to express their opposition to the establishment (Coleman, 1957; Pinard, 1963).

Another important element in such a decision-making process is the organizational structure of the government. Sapolsky (1968) noted that in eight of nine cities with populations of over 500,000 and with a partisan mayor-council form of government, fluoridation was adopted administratively without a referendum. In nine cities of similar population size with nonpartisan or city-manager forms of government, no action on fluoridation had been taken or the government was forced into a referendum on the issue, sometimes more than once. The issue was defeated in seven of eleven referenda. Apparently in large cities where governments are organized with more pervasive political control, city administrations are not forced as often into referenda on controversial issues. However, a study of a much larger sample, more than 1,000 cities, found that the adoption of fluoridation without a referendum occurred more often in cities with a city-manager form of government (Crain, *et al.*, 1969). Thus, it appears that a nonpartisan city manager may be able to manage smaller cities more easily than larger ones.

When issues cannot be settled successfully at the community level, they are often resolved at other levels of government. In

Connecticut, for example, fluoridation was adopted on a state-wide basis as a result of conflicts at the local level. Two cities, Hamden and New Haven, ordered the New Haven Water Company, a private supplier of community water, to fluoridate their water. The company refused to do so and took the matter to court. Since the company supplied water to nine other communities, the court ruled that it could not be required to fluoridate the water of two of the communities by local ordinance. The advisory group to the State Health Department, the Public Health Council, then recommended that all communities over 20,000 population have fluoridated water and a coalition of citizens groups lobbied in the state legislature for a law to implement that policy. Such a law was passed in 1965 and, despite later developing opposition, the law remained in effect in Connecticut (Hirakis, et al., 1967).

The Process of Community Health Planning

As in any system, when communities grow in size and complexity, the individuals, groups, and organizations devoted to one or another aspect of community health also increase in number and their relationships become more complex. Like other aspects of community life in the United States, these elements often proliferate with little or no assessment of the overall needs of the community and of how the community should be organized to meet them. Organizations will usually be initiated or modified to meet particular perceived needs, often without any consideration of this special need relative to the entire pattern of health needs in the community. A religious group may build a hospital in a community while, at the same time, the local government as well as a private group of physicians each plan to build hospitals. Each of these hospitals may have expensive equipment, such as a cobalt machine for certain types of radiation therapy in a community in which one such machine would be more than adequate for the need. Rather than compete on price, which would keep hospitalization costs down, hospitals often compete on the number and variety of services and equipment they offer, thus increasing the overall hospitalization costs of the community (Harris, 1964).

Analogous to the situation that occurred in the case of fluoridation in Connecticut, the lack of coordination and cooperation among governmental and private organizations involved in medical care has become increasingly evident in many communities. The federal government tried to alleviate the situation somewhat through the Medicare-Medicaid legislation, which provided funds to pay for medical care to many families who were unable to do so. However, the infusion of more money into the various medical care systems involved merely accentuated the inefficiencies that had resulted from the lack of coordination.

In the first year of Medicaid and Medicare, the rate of increase of physicians' fees tripled and the rate of increase in hospital fees multiplied five times. It seems obvious that the increase was the result of unrestricted and unplanned allocation of a medical care system without attempting to make the necessary basic changes in its organization, delivery and manpower components (French, 1970).

This is a classic example of unregulated growth in one set of systems pressuring other systems in such a way that they must adapt. State and federal governments have increasingly pressed for local coordination and reorganization of medical care systems. Federal laws providing for hospital construction and special programs for particular diseases contained provisions for planning of medical care facilities and programs on a local and regional basis. However, the laws do not specify who the planning agency shall be or with what authority it can reorganize the system. Without such authority, the planning agencies, where they are formed, can only attempt to bring together the various organizations in the community and try to get them to agree on some coordinated plan.

It will come as no surprise that most individuals will cooperate to coordinate their efforts only when they perceive that it is in their interest to do so. For example, in one case, citizens' groups, physicians, and representatives of various public agencies formed an ad hoc regional medical program planning committee. The citizens' groups were almost exclusively interested in having a physician in each town, although in some towns the population was not large enough to support a physician full time. The physicians came to the meetings "apparently to protect their territory" from other groups, which they usually labeled "socialistic." People representing the public agencies showed willingness to cooperate only when they held some advantage—"those interagency relationships or personal

137

friendships with directors or other echelons of federal and/or state agencies that make it possible to come out with enlarged bureaucracy through additional funds for staff and program" (Harnish, 1969).

This is not to imply that planning agencies or other groups that developed as a result of federal legislation are entirely impotent. The Medicaid program included "leverage" which the health department of New York City used to set standards for providers of medical care. Representatives of public and private hospitals as well as medical care delivery groups and private physicians made up the Medicaid advisory committee. In spite of considerable differences involving ideology and vested interests, the committee was able to devise systems for setting standards for medical care and for auditing those organizations and individuals delivering the medical care (Bellin, 1969).

Perhaps the most important result of legislation calling for planning is that it tends to increase the amount of information about the inadequacies of the various systems involved. The number of information feedback systems is increased among individual members and organizations in the community as well as among the federal agencies responsible for administering legislation. As this information is disseminated, further initiatives for coordination and possibly reorganization of community health services should be forthcoming. Many of these initiatives will originate in state or federal government. The next chapter discusses the organization of these governments relevant to health and also deals with the politics of implementing changes in health-related areas.

8
The societal level: services, regulation, and research

The federal government is the vortex of societal-level decisions that bear on the health of the people in the United States. The federal government has four fundamental roles in health and medical care:

(1) provision of health care, health care financing, or other health-related services to designated segments of the population; (2) promulgation of regulations and standards related to health-care delivery and to products and activities of organizations and individuals that are potentially injurious or efficacious to the health of the citizenry; (3) support of health-related research and education in universities, profit-making and nonprofit research organizations, and within the government itself; (4) the negotiation of relationships and programs with foreign governments and international organizations that affect health and welfare of all the people on the earth.

We shall deal with the first three of these roles in this chapter and the fourth in the following chapter. Before proceeding to that, however, a brief discussion of the organization of the federal government and the process of governmental decision-making is necessary.

Organization of the Federal Government

The Constitution provides the authority and limitations on the authority of the federal government. It is sufficiently ambiguous to allow considerable leeway in governmental action and, at the same time, to result in momentous legislative and legal Donnybrook Fairs over certain policies and issues. The Constitution does not mention health specifically but a number of clauses and amendments define the governmental authority appropriate to the protection of the "general welfare" of the people. The authority to regulate interstate commerce, levy taxes, and to operate the postal service has evolved to include the regulation of food, drugs, and other products potentially toxic or injurious. The authority to grant patents allows for some regulation of new drugs and other products. International health-related activities are conducted under the authority to make war and international treaties. The authority to create agencies and to appropriate money for the general welfare is important in almost all of the federal activities related to health (Anderson, 1969).

The executive, legislative, and judicial branches of the federal government are, constitutionally, separate and equal. In this century, however, the executive branch by the nature of its authority to implement policy has grown in size, complexity, and in specialized expertise to the point that most proposals for governmental policy begin there. At times Congress does not approve the President's policies and, occasionally, may initiate a policy not desired by the President when it can muster a two-thirds majority to override a Presidential veto. A reluctant President faced with an unwanted mandate from Congress can sometimes find ways of molding the program to suit his aims. But, as with any manager of a bureaucracy, a President may have difficulty in gaining compliance to his wishes by all civil servants, particularly among those with strong congressional support. The courts resolve conflicts among branches of government and other parties when and if the issue is taken to court and the judiciary decides that the case merits a hearing. Since the people eligible to vote elect the President and the Congress, who in turn, respectively, appoint and confirm the judiciary, there is a degree of popular control (feedback) of governmental policy.

A number of consequences of this governmental structure should be pointed out. As in the case of local communities and states, organized groups that can deliver campaign contributions and/or influence large blocks of votes usually have more influence on elected governmental officials than do individual voters. For example, governmentally financed and delivered medical care for veterans of the armed services no doubt partially resulted from gratitude for service rendered to the country. However, it is doubtful that such a health program would have been initiated and would have grown without the well-organized lobbying efforts of veteran's organizations, particularly in view of the opposition to parts of the program by another well-financed and organized lobbying group, the American Medical Association (Lewis, 1970). Lobbying is often viewed as somewhat distasteful at best, and corrupt at worst. Yet it exists in one form or another in the politics of all organizations, private as well as governmental, and is only corrupt when the issue turns on the basis of favors rather than consideration of the merits of the issue.

Governmental policies can be characterized as distributive, regulatory, and redistributive (Lowi, 1964). The viability of each of these types of policies is a function of the economic and social conditions prevalent at the time. Distributive policies are more often acceptable when resources are readily available and must be divided. When the country was expanding territorially as well as in times of rapid economic expansion, distributive policy was the most common form of government policy. If the government is giving away, or selling at low cost, previously unclaimed land, or building hospitals, dams, military bases, and highways, the problem is: Who gets what? The policy is usually implemented on a case-by-case basis rather than by general regulations and much trading of contents of the "pork barrel" occurs.

Regulatory policies tend to come to the fore as resources become limited and the distribution or use of particular sets of limited resources is seen as being abused or having the potential for abuse. "Natural" monopolies such as railroads and utility companies were the first to be regulated. The chartering of corporations by the states and the court rulings that these organizations had the same legal rights as individuals resulted in the growth in corporations of national and international scope (Anderson, 1962). Small businesses could systematically be singled out and undersold to the point of ruin at minimal loss to a large corporation. The resultant tendency toward monopoly and subsequent disregard for the public interest in the quality of products and delivery of services, and their prices, led to increased regulatory policies by government. These types of policies tend to be applied more or less uniformly to broad segments of industry, labor, and commerce rather than being decided on a case-by-case basis (Lowi, 1964).

Redistributive policies are demanded in a situation in which resources are relatively scarce and the have-nots and/or groups oriented toward equitable distribution perceive their maldistribution. Some degree of redistribution of resources may occur in many distributive and regulative policies, but often subtly and not necessarily from the haves to the have-nots. Deliberate policies to take from one segment of society and give to another are sufficiently different to warrant a class of their own.

The nature of each of these types of policies affects the type of coalitions formed to effect them, the degree of conflict involved in the decision-making process, and their prospects for implementation or continuance. Because of the case-by-case distribution and the option to trade votes or support on different policies, coalitions formed around distributive policies tend to be stable, conflict is minimal, and implementation is limited only by availability of funds or other resources.

Regulative policies tend to involve shifting, less stable coalitions because different sets of individuals or groups may have different interests depending on the policy. For example, a company with a patent on a safety device that the government proposes to require on all products of a type, such as a shield on a cutting blade, may not join another company, to whom it could sell the device, in opposition to the regulation. Because of the conflicts in interests and the lack of stable coalitions, regulative policies involve considerable conflict and, through eventual compromise, often are reduced to the lowest common denominator, that is, less than adequate regulation in the public interest.

Redistributive proposals tend to result in two stable coalitions of supporters and opposers. The conflict is often rancorous, with little room for compromise (Lowi, 1964). Because elected government officials often have constituencies on both sides of the issue, they tend to delay action as long as possible. Often, in fact, they take no action in order to avoid alienating either side, although some alienation results from such inaction. Some redistributive policies, such as the graduated income tax, have been implemented, but the loopholes negotiated in compromise have softened the impact on the losing side considerably. In some cases, these loopholes have resulted in bringing about even greater discrepancies in distribution.

These general principles are overlaid with patchworks of ideology regarding the nature of man and the proper role of government, and with the personal idiosyncracies and abilities of policy makers and those who attempt to influence them. Once a policy is made official, its implementation becomes the responsibility of a newly created or existing executive department or independent regulatory agency that must work out the nuts and bolts of the everyday application of the policy. The effectiveness of any policy depends on sufficient appropriations from Congress, the abilities and expertise of the appointed administrators, and the cooperation between related governmental agencies and the societal elements that are affected by it. We can hardly provide a complete exposition of all these factors on health-related policies of the federal government. Some illustrations should point to their role in a few important areas.

Governmental Process in Medical Care Financing and Services

The most controversial of the federal government's activities in health has been its increased involvement in the direct provision of, or the financing of, medical care for individual citizens. Yet the practice is not without precedent.

Almost from its inception, the federal government was involved in the financing and delivery of medical services. Following a British tradition (established after the battle with the Spanish Armada), some of the founding states of the United States started "Marine Hospitals" in port cities to care for ill or disabled seamen. In 1798, Congress imposed a tax on seamen's pay to support these hospitals. In 1801 the government purchased a Marine Hospital from the state of Virginia; other such purchases followed later as well as the construction of a hospital in Charlestown, Massachusetts. These activities were the precursors of what became the Public Health Service (Williams, 1951).

Medical care for veterans began in federally supported homes in the early nineteenth century. Public Health Service Hospitals also provided care for veterans over the years until a separate agency, The Veterans Bureau, was authorized by statute in 1921. As is common in bureaucratic systems it was reorganized into the Veterans Administration (VA) in 1930. By 1965, 171 VA hospitals served more than 700,000 patients per year from a potential pool of about 22 million eligible veterans (Lewis, 1970).

These developments were not without opposition. The original debate over the Marine Hospitals involved the question of whether or not seamen were truly needy. Similar questions have been raised regarding veterans, especially in regard to care for problems not associated with military service. Proponents of such care argued that veterans were deserving regardless of their ability to pay, and were successful in implementing the policy in the face of strong opposition from the American Medical Association (Lewis, 1970).

Building of government hospitals is a distributive policy and the conflict over such a pork-barrel measure is likely to be minimal until redistributive or regulatory issues are involved. As long as the recipients, seamen and veterans, paid for the services, either directly through taxes or indirectly through service, the opposition to the policy was relatively ineffective. However, opposition has increased as care for nonservice-related disability (redistributive) and standards for quality of the care delivered (regulatory) have increased.

Complete equity in the distribution of medical services is unlikely although there are prospects for some redistribution (Fein, 1972). The attempts to achieve such equity in the United States is a classic case of the politics of redistributive policy. There were some unsuccessful attempts at legislation of "model medical care insurance" in a few states from 1915 to 1918, but federal action was not seriously considered until much later. Only in 1934, in the midst of a devastating economic depression when overnight many "haves" had become "have-nots," was a directive to study health insurance attached to the original Social Security bill. It was quickly dropped for fear of jeopardizing the entire legislation. After World War II, President Harry F. Truman's Commission on the Health Needs of the Nation wrote that "Access to the means of attainment and preservation of health is a basic human right" (Marmor, 1970). The American Medical Association promptly imposed a $25 levy on each member to finance a lobbying campaign against any legislation for national health insurance.

In succeeding years rancorous debate raged in Congressional committees over the issue. Because of the popularity of the social security system, proponents of a federal health insurance program changed their strategy to focus on the elderly, to be run by the existing Social Security Administration. Neither the administration of President Dwight D. Eisenhower nor the Republican-Southern Democratic coalition in the Congress (based on pork barrel trading and overlap in ideology) were sympathetic, and no health insurance legislation passed in the 1950's. A compromise bill providing for matching grants to the states for medical care insurance programs for the aged was legislated in 1960, but few states chose to implement such programs (Marmor, 1970).

On a nationwide basis, programs based on matching federal and state funds may widen rather than narrow inequities. Wealthier states are in a better position to provide matching funds than poorer states. However, such compromises appeal to supporters of states rights or limitation of federal government.

The administration of President John F. Kennedy proposed a national health insurance program for the aged, but the House Ways and Means Committee was composed of a majority of conservative members and a chairman who had co-authored the previous state-matching program. The bill died in committee. However, the balance of power in the committee and the Congress generally was shifted by the overwhelming Democratic Party victory in 1964. Only then, in 1965, could the Medicare-Medicaid legislation, providing payment for a proportion of the medical care of the aged and certain low-income families with dependent children, be enacted (Marmor, 1970). This was done in spite of the $1 million spent by the AMA in the first quarter of 1965 alone in lobbying efforts against the bill (Rayack, 1967).

The role of the AMA in opposition to these programs has been interpreted as largely a result of the obsessive protection of

145

professional prerogatives and to the protection of their economic advantages (Rayack, 1967). But net physician income increased at an average of over 10 percent per year in the five years after the enactment of Medicare-Medicaid (Marmor, 1970). A national compulsory health insurance program probably would help physician income, yet the AMA favors a voluntary program (Berki, 1972). Reaction to the potential regulation of practice and the AMA's role as spokesman for the most traditional and conservative segments of the profession are more likely explanations of its positions.

The influence of conservative Congressmen in the delay of national health care legislation cannot be attributed entirely to AMA lobbying nor can their elections be attributed entirely to AMA-based campaign contributions. According to one political analyst, the AMA influenced the debates but not the decisions. "The fight centered on whether the redistribution was warranted (were the aged needy enough?), the instrument of change (charity or insurance) and the sources of finance (general revenues or social security taxes). This redistribution frame of reference determined the shape of conflict, not the uncertain scale of redistribution that would in fact be involved" (Marmor, 1970). The role of feedback to Congressmen from constituents experiencing ever-increasing medical care costs is less well documented but it was undoubtedly a factor.

The uncertainty of the redistributive aspects of any policy lies in the extraordinary complexity in accounting for the flow of resources and benefits in current U.S. tax structure and programs. In addition, there is no absolute scale of who is deserving of what benefits according to his contribution.

The Process of Health-Related Government Regulation

Rivaling the financing and delivery of health services for leadership in "the most controversial" sweepstakes is the governmental promulgation of regulations and standards for services and products that have an effect on health. As we have noted, standards for and regulation of medical practice by government conflicts with the notion that a profession has the autonomy to regulate itself. Similarly, governmental setting of standards and the regulation of the production and sale of products and services is in conflict with the norm of free enterprise. Although it will not be found on any death certificate, one could observe that many deaths occur indirectly from professional autonomy and free enterprise.

The U.S. Constitution was not intended as justification for completely free enterprise. It clearly allowed for regulation of private enterprise under certain conditions for the general welfare. This is not to say that such regulation is always effective in promoting the general welfare.

In the U.S. the ideological orientation toward free enterprise and the controversial nature of regulatory policy usually results in a reluctance on the part of government officials to regulate until a situation becomes acute. There seems to be a process in which self-regulation of an industrial, professional, or other group is attempted first in a trade or professional association. However, profitability tends to take precedence over safety and efficacy in such situations. When self-regulatory procedures obviously fail to control abuses, those suffering the abuse, whether groups or individuals, may attempt to apply sanctions by boycott or other means. Usually, however, they look to the government for help.

Feedback from the governed to the government occurs as muckraking writers expose the abuses and congressional hearings are held, not necessarily in that order. Sometimes the regulatory legislation is passed at this time, but often a widely publicized flagrant abuse or tragedy provides the catalyst that moves the government to action. Although not a test of the generality of these assertions, a few examples should illustrate the process.

In early America the "snake oil" salesmen toured the countryside selling nostrums "guaranteed" to heal every malady imaginable. Though knowledgeable pharmacists were also available, the quality of their drug supplies was guaranteed only by their own personal standards and those of their suppliers. Until the Civil War few states and communities had laws regarding drugs, and these were usually aimed at "willful or fraudulent adulteration," a charge difficult to prove. In 1848 Congress enacted a law directing the Secretary of the Treasury to provide for the inspection of imported drugs, but the examiners were often chosen on the basis of their political connections rather than their pharmacologic expertise (Sonnedecker, 1970).

By 1900 most states had drug laws modeled after these

147

earlier ones. However, the ineffectiveness of these laws was exposed by the AMA's Council on Pharmacy and Chemistry, established in 1905. Only about half of the preparations considered by the Council between 1905 and 1907 were approved for use by physicians. Accompanied by Upton Sinclair's muckraking book, *The Jungle,* and a series of articles by Samuel Hopkins Adams in *Colliers,* these findings led to passage of the Pure Food and Drugs Act of 1907 (Burrow, 1970).

A major proponent (and subsequent administrator) of the federal effort was interested mainly in foods, and so drugs tended to be neglected for a time. There was some action against such nostrums as Sporty Days Invigorator, a "male-weakness remedy," and those advertised with "panacea claims" such as Humbug Oil. However, the U.S. Supreme Court upheld a claim "that the law's taboo on false and misleading statements was not intended to apply to therapeutic claims," blunting vigorous government efforts (Young, 1970).

The AMA Council continued its efforts and was an important element in the control of dangerous drugs in subsequent decades. The expansion in the drug industry and the diversion of AMA resources to the opposition of governmental financing and delivery of medical services eventually reduced the AMA's effectiveness in drug evaluation (Dowling, 1970). The increasing profitability of drug advertising in AMA journals may have also been a factor (Silverman and Lee, 1974).

In the late 1920's and early 1930's a series of muckraking books, called the "guinea pig books" because of the common use of such animals in drug experiments, charged that the entire population was being used as guinea pigs in experimentation with drugs and food additives. A new and stronger food and drug bill was drafted in 1933, but powerful lobbies opposed it. President Franklin D. Roosevelt was sympathetic but reluctant to press for passage when legislation needed for recovery from economic depression was considered of highest priority. The bill was not passed until 1938 and then only after public reaction to the deaths of more than 100 people from a solvent used by one manufacturer in a sulfa drug called sulfanilamide (Jackson, 1970).

The 1938 Food, Drugs and Cosmetics Act allowed for

148

regulation of drugs on the basis of their safety but not on the basis of their efficacy. Although the Federal Food and Drug Administration was able to link safety and efficacy in some cases, it was not until 1962, after more muckraking, Congressional probes, and publicity accompanying the birth in a number of countries of thousands of maimed children whose mothers had taken a tranquilizing drug, thalidomide, during pregnancy, that an amendment providing for evaluation of efficacy was passed. It was the safety rather than the efficacy of thalidomide that was the problem, but the tragedy no doubt affected the passage of the tougher amendments regarding drug regulation (Lasagna, 1970). Thalidomide's use in the U.S. had been delayed by the inadequacy of an application to the Food and Drug Administration and its use was limited to a few experimental clinical trials (Silverman and Lee, 1974).

Similar processes have precipitated government regulation in other areas. The death and injury toll associated with motor vehicles mounted for more than 50 years before serious federal action was taken. In spite of the evidence accumulated by scientists and engineers that these losses could be reduced by managing the energy transfer to the human organism in crashes, state and private attempts were limited to attempts to influence human behavior through licensing, driver education, and laws. In most cases the efficacy of the latter efforts had not been subjected to adequate scientific evaluation (Haddon, Suchman, and Klein, 1964). Congressional hearings on the matter began in 1964, and a muckraking book on the subject by a young lawyer, Ralph Nader, became popular the following year. However, it was not the issue itself but the revelation in early 1966 that an automobile manufacturer had kept Nader under surveillance by a private detective and the public apology of the company's president before a U.S. Senate committee, that focused public attention on the issue. The National Traffic and Motor Vehicle Safety Act and the Highway Safety Act became law a few months later, providing respectively for safety standards in the manufacture of motor vehicles and standards, as well as grants-in-aid, for state programs (McCarry, 1972).

Whether muckraking, tragedy, or scandal are necessary conditions for regulatory legislation is open to question. Presidents and Congressional leaders have staffs who may keep them informed of societal problems and can gain expertise on any issue from almost any resource in the society. The numbers and complexity of the issues with which these leaders must deal, however, tend to result in concern with only those issues that are provoking a crisis in the system. Experts in the departments and independent regulatory agencies of government, as well as in the society at large, may anticipate problems and make recommendations, but it is often not easy to get the attention of the policy making level of government, particularly when powerful industries or other groups lobby against regulation.

The success of Ralph Nader as a symbol of citizen action coupled with the increased concern over health, safety, and the environment resulted in a number of new citizen-sponsored organizations that operated under such terms as consumer advocates, citizen's lobbies, and public interest advocates. Passage in rather quick succession of a number of pieces of regulatory legislation in the late 1960's can be attributed at least partially to the efforts of one or more of these groups. Legislation regarding wholesale meats, natural gas pipeline safety, radiation control, coal mine health and safety, and comprehensive occupational health and safety indicates their range of concern. However, the sacrifices in life style necessary to conserve energy and provide a safe, clean environment are only beginning to be felt. Whether the various groups involved in this effort can retain their support remains to be seen (Leone, 1972).

New regulatory legislation may give new authority to an existing governmental department or may direct that a new agency be created to promulgate and administer the new standards and regulations. Sometimes the legislation contains specific standards and rules, but more often only their broad outlines are indicated and the specific rules to implement the legislation are made by the administrative agency. For example, the National Traffic and Motor Vehicle Safety Act of 1966 directed that safety standards be promulgated for new vehicles and equipment manufactured for sale in the U.S. Specific standards were left to the new agency, now the National Highway Traffic Safety Administration, but it was specified that the standards be based on "performance" rather than "design" criteria. In other words the agency could not tell the vehicle manufacturers how to design the vehicles, but it was to set minimum criteria for vehicle performance in protecting people from injury both in and outside the vehicles (Haddon, 1972).

A regulatory agency must follow certain procedures in its rulemaking. A notice of rulemaking must be published in the *Federal Register,* and a particular time period must be allowed for public comment and possible revision of the rule. Occasionally, some member of Congress may not like the proposed rule and may attempt to override it through legislation or informal pressures. When the Federal Trade Commission proposed a rule calling for the "hazardous to your health" warning in cigarette advertising and on cigarette packages, opposition from powerful congressmen, especially from tobacco-growing states, resulted in a compromise whereby the labels were placed on the packages but not in advertising (Fritschler, 1969). Later, when the Federal Communications Commission (FCC) proposed that cigarette advertising on radio and television be banned, the House Interstate and Foreign Commerce Committee reported out a bill effectively countermanding the FCC action; however, the bill was not enacted and the advertising was banned.

Perhaps the most powerful weapon of Congress is control of an agency's budget. The Food and Drug Administration's budget was cut from $5.6 million in 1953 to $5.2 million in 1954 because a constituent of the chairman of the House Appropriations Committee complained when the FDA ruled him in violation of the law for cutting large beets into small round pieces and selling them as the more desirable baby beets (Cavers, 1970).

Although there are some wins and some losses for the overall public welfare in these processes, the checks and balances provided by multiple centers of power and the dependence of the Congress and the President on public support tends to keep the government somewhat responsive to that welfare. The lack of comprehensive strategies for a more responsive government that was revealed in the five major studies of independent regulatory commissions since 1937 has been denounced (Bernstein, 1972). Yet, given the controversial nature of regulatory policy and the crosscurrents of interests involved, it is doubtful that such strategies can be devised without giving so much authority to one or another group that there would be little guarantee against its abuse.

151

The Process of Government-Supported Research and Education

The federal government provides about two-thirds of the money for scientific research in the United States. Since the eventual impact of many scientific projects on the future health of the nation's citizens is not always evident, it is not possible to attribute the proportion of the amount spent that is health-related. Approximately three-fourths of the governmental expenditures for science are handled by defense, space, and atomic energy agencies. At least 11 departments or agencies of the government do health-related research (Carey, 1968).

Whether or not results of research will be used for the health of all the people, for only selected groups of people, or for ill, is a political rather than a scientific question. Some scientists are also politicians, in the broad sense of that word, and, therefore, have considerable influence on research policy and the eventual use of the research results.

Scientists serve on advisory committees to executive governmental agencies, confer privately with members of Congress, testify before congressional committees, and hold positions in agencies that do research or expend research funds. About two-thirds of all governmental research funds are spent in private industry, with about 20 percent going to government laboratories and 13 percent to universities and other nonprofit agencies (Carey, 1968). The pork barrel principle is at work in a considerable proportion of the allocation of research funds. Congressmen and senators announce the awarding of large research contracts and grants to industries, universities, or other organizations in their districts. Charts are drawn up showing the geographic distribution of research funding in particular agencies, and some effort is made to keep the distribution balanced.

The balancing of research funding on the basis of geographic distribution or the allocation of funds on the basis of the interests in a program by a President or politically strong Congressional leader does not necessarily result in a balanced scientific program either in terms of the welfare of the population or the state of the art in a field of science. Noting these problems, some scientists have advocated a department of science at the Cabinet level to coordinate and administer a more balanced governmental scientific program (Brooks, 1968). Whether such a department could accomplish these ends is problematic. With the pork barrel principle and the strong current support of the Department of Defense and the National Aeronautics and Space Administration (NASA) in Congress and in certain industries, it appears doubtful that a science department would be formed in the forseeable future.

The major outlet for biomedical research expenditures in the federal government has been the National Institutes of Health, organizationally a part of the U.S. Public Health Service which is an echelon of the Department of Health, Education, and Welfare. Although the Institutes, as individually created, bore the names of broad clinical disease categories such as Cancer and Mental Health, their "broad mission" was basic research. By performing research to determine the fundamental nature of human biology, or animal biology where human studies were not feasible, scientists believed that they would make discoveries that would result in applications to the control of disease (Wooldridge, *et al.,* 1965). This policy and the increases in funds during the 1950's and 1960's to implement it were remarkably free of the controversy that has characterized policies regarding delivery of services and regulation.

Federal funding of biomedical research increased from $27 million in 1947 (Wooldridge, *et al.,* 1965) to $2.5 billion in 1968, remaining at about that level yearly into the early 1970's (Strickland, 1971). In addition to the pork barrel nature of research expenditures, the relative lack of controversy over these appropriations can be attributed to the broad consensus in the goal of conquering disease among the population and the enthusiasm for these research programs on the part of important Congressional leaders. This enthusiasm was so strong that, during the period of rapidly increasing budgets, Congress sometimes appropriated more money for the National Institutes of Health than had been requested.

Some of the congressmen's enthusiasm for research probably resulted from their desire to support health-related activities and their wish to avoid the controversies in the federal support for health services and medical education (Strickland, 1971). The AMA was almost as strongly opposed to government support of medical education as it was to such direct support of medical care. Although the AMA's opposition to federal support of medical education was claimed to be based on fear that the government would attempt to control the content of the education, it was more likely based on the desire to limit the number of physicians in practice to maintain the economic advantages of the relative lack of competition (Rayack, 1967).

The scientific programs of the National Institutes of Health have been remarkably free of governmental control of their content. Emphasis on broad categories of disease has been affected somewhat by budget allocations. Guidelines were promulgated for such important policies as informed consent of humans involved in experiments and the care of experimental animals; however, the research ideas and methodologies to pursue them have not been matters of governmental policy. Evaluation of research proposals has been accomplished by a system of "peer review" in which scientists working on related problems served on committees as government consultants to judge the proposals' relative merits (Wooldridge, *et al.*, 1965).

There has been some mutual back-scratching and poor science in this system. However, the alternatives of governmental specification of scientific policy, based on ideology or some other criterion, is not attractive as can be seen from experience in other countries. In the Soviet Union, for example, research in genetics was crippled for a time by Lysenkoism, so named after a plant breeder who claimed that genes were modified by experience rather than by mutation. This theory was in line with communist ideology regarding social determinants of human behavior. Lysenko rose to prominence in the Soviet government and led purges against scientists whose theories and experimental evidence contradicted the party line (Gardner, 1957).

The strong governmental emphasis on biomedical research, accompanied and perhaps exacerbated by lack of governmental action in regard to medical care delivery and medical education, nevertheless had an effect on the latter two areas (Strickland, 1971). The sophisticated technology developed as a result of the research was expensive, and the patient unfortunate enough to find himself in need of this technology often was helped medically but ruined financially. Many patients simply could not afford certain kinds of expensive treatment. The manpower to deliver services was also attenuated by the research effort. The physicians who became researchers rather than practitioners were not replaced sufficiently. While the faculties of medical schools tripled in size in 20 years, the number of students enrolled increased by less than 20 percent (Strickland, 1971).

By the mid-1960's many, if not most, of the faculties of medical schools were primarily engaged in federally supported research. One-half to two-thirds of medical school budgets, depending on the school, were financed by federal research funds. These funds, rather than being a boon to the educational goals of these schools, often undermined them. This was especially true in the case of producing skilled practitioners. The students often received fragmentary education by researchers who each gave a few lectures a year and rushed back to their laboratories. Perceiving that prestige and other rewards went to researchers, many students followed their mentors to the laboratories. Only the most conscientious faculty members took the time and effort to assist students in the assimilation and integration of knowledge needed for the rigors of medical practice.

These results did not occur because of a deliberate governmental policy planned toward that end, nor do we mean to imply that most biomedical researchers deliberately avoided the education of students. There is no reason why an affluent society should not support a strong biomedical research effort. The imbalance toward research in the traditional medical school triumviate of service, teaching, and research resulted from the tendency of governmental leaders to prefer the easily negotiated and implemented distributive policies to the much tougher problems of redistribution and regulation.

9
International perspectives

If redistributive and regulatory policies are difficult to enact within one nation, they are even more so on the international level. Some societies have managed more equitable distribution of medical services and other health-related activity than the United States; others have done less; but many have had little to distribute, much less redistribute.

There has been some redistribution of wealth among countries through international aid of various types. Some efforts were directly related to health, but some, such as military aid, may offset the effects of aid for health or welfare. Military weapons seldom improve anyone's health. International regulations have contributed to the control of diseases but the failure of international regulation of war has had devastating effects on the health of large populations, both directly as a result of battle and genocidal policies and indirectly through the increased disease rates that accompany war.

In this chapter we shall briefly note some of the health and medical care systems in selected countries. We will conclude with a discussion of some international efforts and prospects for the future health of the world's population.

National Health Care Systems

Comparison of countries is a precarious business. Countries may be alike in some respects for different reasons. Differences among countries on health or other indicators are often taken as evidence of the superiority of one social system over another, without a careful analysis of the reason for the differences, or consideration of other intersocietal differences that would not support the same conclusion. For example, in the 1950's it was popular in some circles in the United States to assert that a relatively capitalistic democracy such as the U.S. was superior to a relatively socialistic democracy such as Sweden because the reported Swedish suicide rate was higher than the reported rate in the U.S. The difference, however, was less than a factor of two and could have resulted from cultural differences in willingness to report suicide on official death certificates. Causes of death that involve social stigma or family embarrassment are sometimes not accurately reported (Haberman, 1969).

Also, although the difference in suicide rates between the two countries was small, reported homicide rates were 17 times as high among males and 9 times as high among females in the U.S. compared to Sweden. The reported U.S. rates for cirrhosis of the liver (often indicative of alcoholism) were five times higher among males and seven times higher among females than in Sweden (Rutstein, 1967). Whether suicide, homicide, and alcoholism in a country are functions of its economic system, or of genetic, social, or cultural characteristics, is an interesting topic for research. But the intricacy of the interrelationships of factors that contribute to societal differences is sufficient to render simplistic societal comparisons invalid.

It is more useful to analyze how different societies cope with particular problems, such as the problem of equity in health services (Anderson, 1972). With such an analysis one can question the feasibility and possible consequences of adapting solutions from one society to another with different social and cultural systems.

Systems in Highly Industrialized Countries

Most highly industrialized countries have governmental programs affecting the distribution of and payment for medical

158

services. Many of these programs are redistributive in the sense that medical care is financed through a tax system that requires greater payment by wealthier segments of society. In some cases medical care is free or involves only nominal fees for some or all citizens. The degree of governmental regulation of the organization and distribution of services varies widely.

The United Kingdom (U.K.), the origin historically of many laws and traditions in the United States, has evolved differently from her rebellious child. For the most part in the U.K. the tradition of *noblesse oblige,* long nurtured by the interdependence of nobleman and serf, remained in force with the nobility, particularly in England and Wales. While the Elizabethan Poor Law of 1601 and its revisions in 1834 provided for state and, later, parish responsibility for the destitute, the aristocracy assumed considerable responsibility for the provision of various services to the "deserving poor." Boards of Guardians administered the Poor Laws and used a competitive bidding process to recruit physicians, who were closely supervised to avoid excessive expenditures (Anderson, 1972). Members of the aristocracy founded and substantially financed voluntary hospitals, gaining prestige from serving on their boards and some control over who could be treated in them. Physicians who treated the aristocracy (not in the voluntary hospitals but in homes and other private facilities) often served for no fees in the voluntary hospitals. Later, when these hospitals became centers of physician training, education and service in them came to be seen as a means of acquiring a wealthy and prestigious clientele (Abel–Smith, 1964).

The industrial revolution fostered a middle class of skilled workers who formed mutual benefit groups called Friendly Societies. These groups negotiated with general practitioners, who had not managed to gain positions in voluntary hospitals, to provide medical care for their members on a capitation rather than a fee-for-service basis (Anderson, 1972).

By the beginning of the twentieth century it was becoming increasingly clear that substantial segments of the population were medically neglected. The voluntary hospitals were not distributed geographically to provide access to the maximum number of people, and many excluded persons with certain diseases. Municipal hospitals had developed to care for the destitute, but scientifically based medicine had not breached their walls sufficiently to make chances of survival acceptable to many people. And large segments of the working poor were not in Friendly Societies and had insufficient means to pay private practitioners (Abel–Smith, 1964).

After much debate, the Health Insurance Act was legislated in 1911. It required compulsory insurance for low-income workers, who were guaranteed medical care and drugs when ill. Physicians were not required to participate but most did, over two-thirds of general practitioners doing so by the 1940's. They were paid on a capitation rather than a fee-for-service basis, following the precedent of the Friendly Societies. This became the "backbone of income for most doctors" (Lindsey, 1962). Nearly half the adult population, was so insured by the 1940's, but families of workers were not covered.

World War II placed great strains on the medical care system in the U.K. Physician income was low and the hours were long. Reorganization was favored and many physicians supported proposals for a National Health Service. There was last-minute resistance and the threat of noncooperation was voiced, but the public and Parliament, as well as reform-minded physicians, prevailed. The National Health Service Act became law in 1946. Resistance largely disappeared and by 1948 more than 97 percent of the population, about 94 percent of the dentists, and about 98 percent of general practitioners and pharmacists were participating (Lindsey, 1962).

Participation in the National Health Service is voluntary, and a small private practice continues. The Service is organized so that the family physician is paid a capitation fee for each person in his panel, as well as for such special services as night calls. The patient pays only for a portion of certain special items such as glasses; otherwise, the service is free, financed from general tax revenues. Specialists called consultants practice only in hospitals and see patients on an outpatient or inpatient basis upon referral of the family physician. Family physicians seldom practice in hospitals (Fry, 1969).

Thus, the National Health Service was not a revolutionary change but evolved from long-established traditions in British society. The benevolence of government evolved from the medieval system of *noblesse oblige*. The capitation fee system originated with the Friendly Societies, and the separation of general practice and hospital medicine primarily resulted from the traditional organization of the voluntary hospitals.

The adaptation of the norms and organizational systems of the past to existing conditions occurs even in societies that have experienced violent revolution. For example, in Russia there were rampant epidemics during the Civil War of 1917–23. The victorious Bolsheviks, although claiming that Marxist principles of communism would eventually prevail, formed a strong centralized governmental structure. The worship of Lenin replaced the traditional worship of the Tsars. The secret police, changed little except in personnel from service of the Tsar to service of the Bolsheviks, controlled or eliminated dissidents, including physicians (Field, 1967; Fry, 1969). Because of the epidemics and the need for healthy workers to bring about economic stability, the health of the population had high priority. Centralization of the planning and delivery of medical services was not strongly resisted.

Like other aspects of Soviet society, five-year plans are used to assess needs, set goals, and allocate budgets for the medical care system. The educational system is also controlled by the state and, within limits of resources, the number of physicians is controlled. The Soviet Union graduates about four times as many physicians per year as the U.S. and is approaching twice as many physicians per 10,000 population (24) as the U.S. (15) (Fry, 1969). In spite of strong state control and the large number of physicians, the U.S.S.R. has similar problems to the U.S. in regard to distribution. There are three times as many physicians per capita in the urban as in the rural areas in the U.S.S.R. Newly trained physicians have a two or three year obligation to be assigned to practice by the state, usually in a rural area. But loopholes, such as the right of a married woman not to be separated from her husband (more than 70 percent of the physicians are women), have resulted in a persistent problem in the distribution of physicians.

The problem is somewhat alleviated by the retention of the feldshers, originally army medics who also treated the civilian population under the Tsars, and of midwives. The government is not particularly proud of these traditions, but thousands of feldshers and midwives serve as the first contact for medical services in rural areas (Field, 1967). Most physicians practice in polyclinics, made up of

161

generalists and specialists, that serve districts of 40,000 to 150,000 people. Citizens may go to feldshers, midwives, or physicians outside these clinics in smaller areas of about 4,000 people, called "uchastoks," or may go directly to the polyclinic, which may have responsibility for some uchastoks. Other than nominal fees for certain items, such as glasses, medical care is free. District, regional, and republic hospitals, financed and controlled by the state, are available for particular types of problems that are referred to them from the polyclinics (Fry, 1969; Muller, et al., 1972).

Greater attention is being paid to these and other international comparisons of health care systems in the industrialized countries (Fry and Farndale, 1972; Andrews, 1973; Shenkin, 1973). Increased knowledge of different systems will no doubt lead to some diffusion of particular practices from one social system to another. Two principles seem to be evident in the change of medical care systems. First, such changes often accompany other rapid changes in the social system that accompany such crises as war and economic depression. Second, the changes in a given country's system are likely to be an adaptation of institutions of the past.

Systems in Industrially Developing Societies

While industrialized nations struggle to distribute services equally, many of the industrially undeveloped and developing nations have few medical services at all. Perhaps more than half of the world's population has no access to scientifically based medical care (Bryant, 1969). The less developed countries are faced with choices of whether to devote their severely limited resources to prevention (sanitation, water purification, elimination of insect and animal disease carriers) or to the development of curative medical care systems. While preventive services would be more efficacious in overall effect on disease and mortality rates, their direct relationship to health is often not evident to the citizen who has no physician available when ill. Thus, political pressures for development of curative services are often stronger than those for preventive efforts (Otolorin, 1968).

Governments and private institutions, such as religious missions, have provided limited international aid. This assistance has often been in the form of curative rather than preventive services, because the increased visibility of the curative services has abetted the sponsor's primary goal of conversion to political or religious beliefs. There are more than 3,200 religiously related medical institutions in the developing countries with a combined budget of more than $300 million. The supporting religious bodies contribute less than a third of this amount, most of it coming from local sources. Often the clinics and hospitals are staffed by people unprepared to manage complex organizations. There is little coordination, and even at times competition, among groups of different religious persuasion. Local governments are often frustrated in planning efforts because of these problems (Bryant, 1969).

China, one of the larger of the developing nations, has apparently made great strides in providing preventive as well as curative services. What the Chinese call "Western medicine" was introduced to the country by missionaries in the middle of the nineteenth century (Sidel, 1973). Until most left or were driven out during World War II and the subsequent communist victory in the civil war, missionary groups provided some services and trained local physicians and health workers. However, perhaps primarily because of war and political chaos, the Chinese people until 1949, the year of the communist victory, were plagued with malnutrition and a wide variety of killing and disabling diseases. Western observers with experience in pre-1949 China have recently been allowed return visits and have been greatly impressed with the dramatic reduction in poverty and disease, at least in the areas that they have been allowed to visit (Liang, *et al.,* 1973).

Official governmental statistics and reports as well as reports from governmentally controlled tours must be viewed with caution, but the evidence is sufficient to conclude that China is well on the way to a solution of many of her long-standing health problems. Apparently this has been accomplished through a complex system of organization in which preventive practices have been carried out on a mass scale and an attempt has been made to merge traditional Chinese medicine (including the use of herbs and acupuncture) with Western medicine. Campaigns, such as the "Four Pests Campaign" against flies, rats, sparrows, and mosquitos, were mixed with mass political instruction in which participation in the campaigns was defined as a patriotic duty.

As in most societies, physicians and medical care facilities in China have tended to concentrate disproportionately in the urban areas, but there has been considerable pressure for health professionals as well as other professional and managerial groups to work in the countryside among the workers and peasants, learning from them as well as teaching and providing services (Liang, *et al.,* 1973). Medical care units were organized in parallel with economic and political units such as agricultural communes and worker's production brigades, with at least one hospital in almost all of the nation's 2,000 counties. Each political and economic unit provided the financing for the medical care of its members (Rifkin, 1973). Although receiving some technical help and equipment from the Soviet Union for a time, most of the Chinese effort has been aimed at self-sufficiency.

It is little wonder that other developing nations are impressed by the Chinese example. However, as we have noted in the industrialized countries, wholesale adoption of a system that may be effective in one country with its social and cultural history may not be politically feasible or have the same effect in a society with a different background (Liang, *et al.,* 1973). With an increased exchange of information among countries, perhaps those elements of particular systems that can be shown to be effective can be adapted to other systems.

One attempt to increase information exchange and the number of skills of physicians in a number of developing countries has been through training programs in the wealthier nations. For example, in the United States in the early 1970's about one of every three interns and residents in teaching hospitals was a graduate of a foreign medical school (Dublin, 1972). However, the advantage of this pattern to the developing nations is questionable since large numbers of these physicians do not return to their native countries; over 90 percent of students from some Asian countries remain in the U.S. Because of the restricted output of U.S. medical schools, it has been possible for these physicians to remain in the U.S. after their training. An estimated 12 new medical schools would have to be built in the U.S. to meet the need currently filled by foreign graduates that remain in the U.S., at a cost about equal to the total amount now spent by U.S. public and private sources in medical aid to the countries from which the physicians migrated (Adams, 1968). This is an illustration of a policy that is apparently redistributive foreign aid, but in fact is no such thing. Furthermore, those physicians that do return to their native countries after residencies in U.S. hospitals have often been trained to treat patients with problems seldom encountered in their home countries and are unprepared to diagnose and treat problems that are prevalent there, perhaps a factor in their decisions not to return.

International Systems

In addition to arrangements among pairs or larger groups of countries for aid, and the exchange of information, technology, and students, a number of more wide-ranging international health organizations have evolved to promote these activities and to regulate certain health-related activities. For centuries, the journey to Mecca by Moslems from North Africa, the Middle East, and Asia provided carriers and routes for the spread of lethal diseases such as smallpox, cholera, and bubonic plague. In the mid-1800's a number of countries with interests in the area formed international organizations to attempt control of the spread of these diseases, mainly through quarantine regulations. There were many problems, some technical and some political. Quarantine is of limited or no value in the case of some of the diseases. Countries traded accusations of espionage when political papers were "rummaged" by quarantine officers (Goodman, 1952).

But the principle of international organization was established. The first international conference on public health generally, not limited to quarantine regulations, was held in Brussels in 1852. Nine such conferences were held in the succeeding 50 years. Two problems that have characterized international relations to the present day were often evident in these meetings: denial of culpability for a problem, and resistance to relinquishing elements of national sovereignty to other nations or to an international organization. For example, Great Britain denied for years that cholera was endemic to her colony in India and was spread epidemically by travelers from there. The U.S. proposed in the Washington conference of 1881 that health inspection of ships be done in the port of origin by agents from the country to which the ships were traveling, but there was strong opposition to such a relinquishment of sovereignty. The measure was not adopted (Goodman, 1952).

The establishment of permanent international offices did not occur until the twentieth century. The Pan American Sanitary

165

Organization was formed in the Western hemisphere in 1902, and *l'Office International d'Hygiene Publique* began its work in Paris in 1907. When the Health Organization of the League of Nations was formed in 1923, there were attempts to merge all international health efforts under its aegis. But France did not want to lose *l'Office* and the United States did not ratify the League charter, mainly because of isolationism after World War I, and so these organizations continued working somewhat in parallel until the World Health Organization (WHO) was formed in 1946.

One simple procedural policy was important in the subsequent development of WHO. Most international organizations had a system that required the ratification of policy by member states before it could be implemented. However, the member states of WHO must reject its proposals within a period of time or the proposal becomes policy. Thus, the inertia in decision-making in governmental organizations tended to increase the probability of adoption of policy in WHO (Goodman, 1952; Brockington, 1967).

During the years since 1946 WHO has grown and by the mid-1970's was engaged in health-related activities throughout the world. Its work is carried out with considerable autonomy, although it is affiliated with the United Nations and its general policies are reviewed periodically by the UN General Assembly and its Economic and Social Council. Funding is not through the UN but is paid directly to WHO by member nations, prorated somewhat by ability to pay. WHO has its own assembly, or parliament, made up of representatives of member nations. It is governed between annual meetings by an executive board of 24 persons, eight of whom are replaced on a rotating basis each year. The board and the chief executive officer, the Director-General, are located in Geneva, Switzerland, with a staff of over 4,000 persons. In addition there are six regional offices.

Included in WHO's activities are the traditional technical responsibilities and services to governments. For example, information on epidemics and potential epidemics is assembled and spread rapidly by means of daily bulletins on a worldwide radio network. Important work is done in the international standardization of drugs and knowledge is disseminated through fellowships, research, and publications. Governments, upon request, may receive information on specific topics or technical assistance on a short-term problem, such as a mass campaign against a particular disease, or a long-term problem, such as planning and organizing health services.

Without detracting from WHO's successes, it must be pointed out that its work is severely limited by its small budget and staff relative to the extent of health problems, particularly in the less developed parts of the world. It is estimated that 80 percent of the world's population has been invaded by parasites, is exposed to other dangerous disease agents, or is malnourished. WHO cannot supercede the sovereignty of any country and cannot intervene in a nation's health problems until a country recognizes a problem and requests help. If all the countries that need help were to request it, the staff and budget are so insufficient that WHO could hardly begin to do the job (Brockington, 1967).

The Future

In the last quarter of the twentieth century, the world looks back on a history of the struggle of the human race with nature and the struggle of people against people. It is divided into nation states, each intensely jealous of its sovereignty and some intent on expanding influence if not territory. The means of mass annihilation of human beings have proliferated. The nations with highly developed scientific and industrial bases have harnessed considerable proportions of the physical, chemical, and biological elements of nature. The delusion that control of the rest was only a matter of time became evident at mid-century.

Only more recently have the voices of those who preceived the limits of growth been heard. Human control of the number of human beings and the maintenance of an environment that will sustain human life and health are problematic. The growth of human population, most acute in the developing countries, and the squandering of limited and irreplaceable resources, particularly in the industrially developed countries, threaten the existence and well-being of the human race.

From the origin of the human species to the historical point at which estimates of population size are possible, about 8,000 B.C., the human population had grown to only five million or so. There were about 300 million people on earth by the time of the Roman Empire and a billion people by 1825. The population doubled to two billion in the succeeding hundred years, around 1925, and will have doubled again to four billion in the 1970's (Keyfitz and Flieger, 1968). As we indicated at the outset of this book, a positive feedback system cannot continue without adjustment of related systems, in this case the ecosystems of the planet earth.

At the 1970 growth rate, there will only be standing room on the entire land area of the earth for the population in a little over 600 years. Assuming that the technological problems of converting all the matter on and in earth to food could be solved, at the 1970 growth rate all of the earth would be converted to human flesh by 3527 A.D., at which point life would abruptly stop. There would be nothing left to convert (Hardin, 1973). Given the limits on technology in developing food and processing human wastes, that point obviously will not be approached. The basic question is whether the present growth will be curbed before the ecosystem is destroyed beyond redemption.

To some degree the growth in population can be attributed to success in controlling diseases, particularly those diseases that formerly killed infants and children before they grew old enough to reproduce. This limited success in disease control has been attained only in the last hundred years, primarily in the industrially developed nations. If the means of drastically reducing population growth to at or near zero are not found in the present generation, all medically related gains in alleviating human suffering will be offset many-fold by the suffering to come.

An estimated two-thirds of the world's population does not receive sufficient calories per day and six-tenths, mostly overlapping with the undernourished, receive insufficient amounts of nutrients essential to healthy growth and development, mainly protein. Deficiencies in calories and nutrients not only maim and kill directly but also result in increased vulnerability to disease agents. What would have been a minor illness becomes life-threatening in the severely malnourished individual.

New varieties of grains, the so-called green revolution, delayed widespread starvation for a time in the 1960's, but the ecology of cultivatable land, fertilizers, and water supplies is such that the effect was temporary. Management of the seas in the production and harvesting of food sources can only be an equally temporary measure given the population growth rates (Ehrlich and

168

Ehrlich, 1972). Nationalistic quarrels over fishing rights have begun and current exploitation threatens to destroy existing species.

In the 1960's the population growth rate in some of the industrialized nations began to decline, as it had at earlier times, often in economic depressions and wars. The abandoning of norms against abortion and wider availability of birth control technology may prevent subsequent increases seen after past such declines. Some 25 less developed countries began official governmental family planning programs, and an additional 19 had programs with limited governmental involvement. The remaining countries had only relatively small-scale private efforts or none. The effectiveness of the family planning approach is severely limited by the nature of present birth control technology and religious, social, and economic norms regarding the desirability of children and the use of the technology. Population surveys in many countries reveal that the desired number of children per family is so high that, with the unlikely achievement of completely effective family planning, the growth of populations would continue to the catastrophic ends outlined above.

Because the desired number of children tends to be lower in industrialized countries, many people believe that population will be controlled by increasing industrialization. However, there are not sufficient resources on earth for the nonindustrialized nations to reach the present level of development of, for example, the U.S. (Ehrlich and Ehrlich, 1972). With less than 6 percent of the world's population, the U.S. is consuming about 30 percent of the earth's processed raw materials in the 1970's. Many of these materials are not recyclable, reproducible, or replaceable in any forseeable technical and economic system. Furthermore, the industrial use of some of these materials and the expulsion of toxic materials on land and in water and air threaten the delicate ecology of essential food chains. Species of plants and animals are damaged or wiped out, species that contribute to the sustenance of the earth and sea in the production of foods used by human populations.

The specter of a small group of industrialized nations struggling to maintain a diminishing food supply and standard of living while the rest of the world starves threatens to become a reality. Many of the raw materials necessary to maintain the standard of living in the industrialized nations are no longer available or are fast

169

being depleted in those nations. How long will nations with starving populations but with undeveloped raw materials be willing to give up those materials without demands for redistribution of food and other commodities? How long will the industrialized nations with superior military forces accede to demands of nonindustrialized nations for redistribution in exchange for raw materials without resorting to military conquest to gain the materials? Like the answer to many a rhetorical question, the answer is obvious: not long.

10
Systems analysis and systems engineering

Clearly the health of future populations depends to some degree on our ability to understand the systems involved, ranging from sub-cellular chemical and biological systems to global social systems. It is also clear that tragedies, great and small, will occur before we gain complete knowledge of all the systems involved, if indeed such knowledge will ever be forthcoming. The question before us then is: with the knowledge available, to what degree can the systems be changed to avoid or ameliorate the undesirable consequences of the continued present course of some of these systems?

Without pursuing a lengthy philosophical discussion of means and ends, the problem is one of avoiding undesirable ends without employing undesirable means. It is perhaps easier to gain agreement on what is undesirable than what is desirable. Utopias are as individual as the cognitive processes of those who indulge in utopian thinking. Yet no utopia involves war, disease, injury, disability, hunger and malnutrition, unless they are accepted as part of the uncontrollable elements of the system. But we know how to avoid many of these undesirable ends in specific cases. Putting this knowledge to work in the systems involved, is, however, a major problem.

Another problem is the exacerbation of an undesirable outcome by amelioration of another. For example, control of infant mortality without decreasing the birth rate increases total population size beyond the capacity of environmental and social systems to provide adequate nutrition. In dealing with individual patients in medicine, we find a hierarchy of amelioration of the most immediately undesirable consequences. The five D's—death, disability, disease, discomfort, and dissatisfaction—are attacked in that order. It may be necessary to disable a person to avoid death. It may be necessary to use means that make the person sick for a time in order to avoid disability or death, and so on (Robertson, *et al.*, 1974).

Such a straightforward hierarchy of undesirable means and ends is not evident in many systems. "Give me liberty or give me death" was a stirring phrase that seemed to indicate such a hierarchy, but those who died for others' liberty did not always do so by personal choice. The issue is not one of absolute liberty to live or die, eat or starve, have children or not have children, but involves whose liberty under what circumstances with what eventual consequences (Westman and Gifford, 1973).

The Tragedy of the Commons

Hardin (1968) has posed the problem of individual liberty and ecological destruction as the "tragedy of the commons." In the history of various areas of the world, there have been periods when people shared a common pasture for the feeding of their animals. The "common," now usually a small park found in the center of some cities and towns, was once used for that purpose. The tragedy of the commons was their eventual overgrazing and destruction because each herdsman exercised his freedom to place as many animals on the common as he wished. There was no immediate loss to the individual if he placed additional animals on the common. But, collectively, when all herdsmen did so, edible elements of the ecosystem were destroyed and inedible elements began to dominate, thus making the common unusable for grazing.

With each family system exercising its freedom to breed, consume, and pollute the common ecosystem that sustains life, the earth is rapidly approaching the tragedy of the commons. The choice is not freedom or death. The choice is how much freedom now for each relative to how long before destruction of all. If the abridgment of freedom to breed is accepted as more undesirable than the eventual and not too distant end of the human race, then the die is cast. Wars over scarce resources, disease, malnourishment, and other undesirables that accompany the choice must be accepted in the bargain.

A world opinion survey on the matter is unlikely. And if such a survey were made, it would not decide the issue. The issue will turn on decisions made in systems at various levels, ranging from families to state, national, and world governments. The role of the scientist is to analyze the relevant systems and provide the information and options for knowledgeable decision making. What, then, can we say about the options available in light of what we know about the systems bearing on health?

Causal Processes and Undesirable Results

The conceptualization of many current health problems both by sociologists and medical scientists is sloppy and leads to unwarranted and ineffective ameliorative strategies in research and practice. Consider the following quote from a medical sociology textbook:

> In erecting defenses against chronic diseases, human groups are faced with very different, and in some ways more difficult, problems than are posed by communicable diseases. The causes of many chronic diseases are already known, e.g., tuberculosis and syphilis. For many others, however, like heart disease, cancer, and arthritis, medical knowledge of causes is yet incomplete.
> . . . A substantial explanation of this incomplete knowledge can be traced to the fact that most chronic diseases are the result of multiple causes rather than a single disease agent, as in the case of many communicable diseases (Coe, 1970).

And, from a dean of a prominent school of public health:

> During the past half-century in the United States there has been a remarkable change in the relative importance, in terms of morbidity and mortality, of the acute communi-

173

cable diseases and the chronic or degenerative diseases (Stebbins, 1966).

There are a number of misconceptions in such thinking. First, the fact that a disease lasts for a long time or is degenerative cannot be taken as evidence that it is not caused by a communicable, infectious, or other agent. Indeed the two "chronic" diseases mentioned in the first quote, tuberculosis and syphilis, have communicable, infectious agents in their etiology. To rule out the possibility of such agents in other diseases of presently unknown etiology without sufficient evidence on each one is foolish.

Second, multiple causation is hardly unique to "chronic" diseases. We know of no disease that is presently understood that does not have many factors in its etiology. Numerous factors affect the exposure and susceptibility of the organism or its elements to damage by whatever agents, internal or external. For example, we noted early in this book the system of fleas, rodents, the infectious agent, and human susceptibility in the etiology of bubonic plague, which would ordinarily be called an "acute, infectious" rather than a "chronic" disease. The incidence, severity, and chronicity of any disease is a function of the complex interplay of a number of factors, including the therapy received.

Third, the number of elements or systems in the etiology of a disease does not determine the effectiveness of therapy. The diseases that have been controlled by medical or social intervention were not controlled because they had a single cause. These diseases were controlled because one or more necessary conditions for human damage were found in the systems involved. A necessary condition is one that must be present somewhere in the input or process for the damage to occur, although damage may not always occur in the presence of the condition. For example, although a streptococcus is a necessary condition for particular types of damage, in some cases a streptococcus may be present but, because of other factors, no disease process occurs. However, control or elimination of streptococci results in reduction or elimination of the damage. In the case of bubonic plague, there are a number of necessary conditions, the bacillus, the fleas, certain flea-carrying animals (squirrels as well as rats have been involved), the proximity of animals and fleas to human populations, and the immunological state of the population attacked.

Factors in causal processes can be logically classified into necessary conditions, sufficient conditions, necessary and sufficient conditions, and contributory conditions. A sufficient condition is one that always produces a particular result, but the result may occur from other conditions as well. A guillotine is sufficient to decapitate a person, but it is not the only or even a frequent cause of such injuries. A necessary and sufficient condition is one that must always be present for a particular result to occur and the result always occurs in the presence of that condition. Often it is not an agent per se that is necessary and sufficient to produce a particular result but the concentration of the agent. For example, lead entering a human organism is necessary to produce lead poisoning, and beyond a certain molecular concentration in the organism lead is sufficient to poison anyone. Many factors are neither necessary nor sufficient to result in damage to humans but are contributory conditions; that is, they increase the probability of damage. For example, the probability of a person contracting lung cancer, emphysema, and heart and blood vessel diseases is increased as the number of cigarettes that person smokes per day increases (U.S. Department of Health, Education and Welfare, 1971). However, all heavy smokers do not contract these diseases, at least as they are diagnosed currently. Smoking, therefore, is not a sufficient condition for the diseases presently defined. Also, each of these diseases occurs in people who have never smoked. Therefore, smoking is not a necessary condition for the diseases. Nevertheless, if smoking could be completely eliminated, the incidence and severity of these diseases would be greatly reduced (Robertson, 1968).

The key to control of undesirable outcomes is the identification and control of the necessary conditions for those outcomes. If a necessary condition can be controlled, then by definition the outcome can be controlled. Understanding of the overall structure and process of the systems involved may be interesting and worthwhile, but amelioration can be achieved without complete understanding of the disease and injury processes. For example, if an infectious agent, such as streptococcus, is a necessary condition for particular damage, such damage can be eliminated by eliminating the streptococcus. Understanding all the human and environmental factors that affect exposure and susceptibility to infection is unnecessary. If energy exchange beyond the tolerance of the human organism is a necessary condition for damage in motor vehicle

175

crashes, as it is, then control of energy in the vehicle by such means as cushions that inflate in serious crashes and in the environment by such products as poles that break easily when struck, can be gained without understanding all the human, vehicular, and environmental factors that affect vehicle crashes.

Finding Necessary Conditions

To find the necessary conditions for damage to people requires considerable care in conceptualization of the problem and choice of research methods. If injury control is conceived as a problem of prevention of the events called accidents, as it often has been, then necessary conditions for damaging energy exchange will not be identified because of concentration on factors that precede the energy exchange. If clinical classifications of disease are accepted without question, then the necessary conditions for particular subsets of the problem will not be identified. Historically, the identification and elimination of specific infectious agents has not eliminated entire sets of descriptively defined clinical entities. For example, entire sets of clinically defined conditions such as rashes, genital lesions, and insanity were not eliminated by the discovery and control of treponema pallidum, the infectious agent in syphilis, but significant subsets of these clinical entities were controlled. These subsets were then redefined in terms of the etiologic agent. Patients infected with treponema pallidum are diagnosed as syphilitic, not as having rashes, lesions, or insanity (Haddon, 1968).

The availability of computers facilitates the examination of multiple sets of variables. An increasing number of reports consist of sets of multivariate analyses, employing such statistical methods as multiple correlation and regression, in which large numbers of measured variables are related to some clinical disease classification. The computer can be a powerful tool in the process of examining data, but data gathered indiscriminately and only lightly touched by human thought are unlikely to yield their secrets. Often there is little thought given to the classifications of the disease or injury in question or how particular variables might indicate manipulable necessary conditions. And in many cases, there is an obvious lack of understanding of the basic assumptions implicit in the statistical model being used. For example, a recently reported study applied

176

a discriminant function analysis to social and biological data obtained from persons who subsequently were followed and classified as to development of heart disease (Lehr, *et al.*, 1973). By doing such an analysis, the authors implicitly assumed that heart disease is a homogeneous set of phenomena and that the variables simply add up in their effects on the disease in straight line (linear) relationships. Among 12 "social" and 12 "biological" variables considered in the study, attention was paid to only one possible interaction, difference between religion of parents. No attention was given to the possibility of feedback or other more complex relationships.

It would be astonishing if most of the etiological factors in clinical entities of presently unknown etiology were to be found to fit linear statistical models. A condition that is necessary but not sufficient for a particular effect would by definition not fit such a model. Even if social and behavioral as well as other factors currently under investigation are etiological factors in some diseases, some of the research methods being used may obscure rather than clarify their importance.

In Chapter 2 we noted behavioral factors that are known to be involved in many diseases, particularly in those in which an infectious agent can be transmitted from one person to the next and/or where human behavior influences exposure. Social and psychological stresses probably contribute to lowered resistance to infectious and other damaging agents. And the neuronal and hormonal reactions to such stresses are thought to be major contributing factors to a number of diseases where no external physical, chemical, or biological agents have been found. The list of social and psychological stresses that is most refined in terms of the criteria for developing measurement scales contains 43 items (Holmes and Rahe, 1967). It is nowhere near being exhaustive. To our knowledge, no single psychological or social stress or set of such stresses has been shown to be a necessary condition for any human damage.

It is not enough to show that a given health problem is more or less prevalent in a given social class, age, sex, or racial group, or among persons of a given marital status. Such information may be useful in specifying where to look for specific necessary conditions or where to direct programs when and if such conditions are found. Perhaps it is not too facetious to point out, however, that

177

public health programs are not going to change the sex, age, or race of individuals and it is unlikely that they can modify the social stratification and marital patterns of society. Since correlations of these factors with health problems are usually low and the causal processes are unspecified, even if some such manipulation were possible it would have very limited effect on the problems.

Control of Necessary and Other Conditions

There are many known necessary conditions for human damage that are presently subject to control. The growth of many cancers can be controlled by surgery or other methods if caught in time. Many diseases can be controlled by immunization, but large populations are not immunized. Substantial damage to motor vehicle occupants can be controlled by safety belt use, vehicle design, and road design. Birth rates that result in populations too large to be nourished can be lowered by controlling various conditions necessary for conception or gestation. The control of these conditions involves one or more of the levels of systems we have discussed, ranging from the cell to international arrangements among countries. The implementation of efficacious strategies, however, requires some rethinking of what is known about these systems.

We noted in Chapter 3 the emphasis on changing attitudes and beliefs as a prerequisite for changing individual health and illness behavior. Yet changes in attitudes and beliefs did not occur in conjunction with increased immunizations of children in a comprehensive care clinic or among women's use of cervical cytology clinics when compared to appropriate control groups. Films and television messages had little or no effect on such behaviors as dieting, exercise, and safety belt use. Two factors, not yet adequately separated by research, appeared to have a significant effect on health and illness behavior: the degree to which the appeal to change behavior was personalized and the frequency with which the behavior was required for individual protection. One strategy, the development of health services that guarantee a personalized, continuous relationship between health professionals and potential patients, would undoubtedly change some health and illness behaviors. However, the many kinds of behaviors involved in various types of human damage and the frequencies with which some of the undesirable behaviors occur suggest that reliance on personal health services alone is insufficient to ameliorate many types of damage.

A second strategy, law or administrative directive, has had reasonable success in affecting some health and illness behaviors. Immunization levels would undoubtedly be lower if certain immunizations were not required for school enrollment, obtaining visas for travel to certain countries, and the like. Australia was the first country to have laws requiring safety belt use, and, during the initial year in Australia at least, the law had substantial effect. Observed belt use was above 60 percent in rural areas and 70 percent in urban areas in the first year after the laws went into effect (Foldvary and Lane, in press), compared to 5 percent to 25 percent in the U.S. (Robertson, *et al.,* 1972). This resulted in a 20 percent reduction in fatalities among vehicle occupants. In the U.K., after certain changes in the laws regarding driving while intoxicated, reductions in motor vehicle fatalities and injuries were observed. However, three years later the fatality rates had returned almost to the levels one would have expected had no change occurred (Ross, 1973). Administrative directives in some organizations require that workers in hazardous areas wear protective equipment, some require periodic physical examinations, and a few even have required exercise periods.

Laws and administrative directives regulating most individual health behaviors are unlikely to be enacted, and many are unlikely to be effective if enacted. For example, a complete ban on smoking could result in the type of large-scale criminal behavior that occurred when alcohol was prohibited in the 1920's and early 1930's, and is occurring with respect to marijuana and other drugs now. Legal and administrative regulation of some individual health related behaviors such as eating is incomprehensible.

There is strong precedent in the strategies of preventive medicine and injury control for approaches alternative to persuasive attempts at individual behavior change or legal and administrative regulation of each individual's behavior. These approaches have been appropriately termed "passive," indicating that the person being protected plays no "active" role in initiating the protection (Haddon and Goddard, 1962). Milk is pasteurized and water is purified to kill bacteria; water is in some instances fluoridated to lower tooth decay; salt is iodized to prevent goiter; cars are required to be manufactured with energy-absorbing steering assemblies and energy-absorbing windshields; and electrical cables are shielded to control certain energy forces, all before they are used by the individual.

Passive strategies have even been found effective in situations where behavior was deliberately directed toward self-destruction. In Birmingham, England, there was a marked reduction in suicides involving domestic coal-gas that paralleled the reduction of the carbon monoxide content of the gas. Although there was a slight increase in suicide by males (but not females) using other methods, there was an overall net reduction in suicides (Hassall and Trethowan, 1972). Numerous examples of presently unused and potential strategies, both active and passive, have been detailed, mainly in the area of damage from various forms of energy (Haddon, 1970; Baker, 1973).

Although it may not be possible to apply a passive strategy to amelioration of all hazards to health, these strategies are clearly preferable to those aimed at individual behavioral change because of their relative sureness and the inherent difficulty in changing individual health behavior. Figure 10–1 provides a logical framework in which to classify public health strategies, both active and passive, by frequency of behavior required by the person being protected. A few examples are given as illustrations.

Individual behavior change strategies are never certain in the sense that the entire relevant population is protected. A survey of immunization of children one to four years of age show that less than 80 percent have obtained DPT (diphtheria, pertussis, and tetanus vaccines combined), poliomyelitis, or measles vaccines (Immunization Survey, 1971). Fortunately, the percentages obtained are usually adequate to keep the incidence of the diseases at a minimum. In a state where a law specified that parents of minor children must present certification of adequate immunization against diphtheria, tetanus, pertussis, rubeola, rubella, smallpox, and poliomyelitis as well as a tuberculin test upon initial entry into school, DPT was the only immunization found in over 80 percent of the relevant population in a follow-up survey. Also, public health clinics did not have sufficient notice and the medical care system was overloaded for a time (Jackson and Carpenter, 1971).

After considerable effort, using various means of persuasion, an increase in cervical cytology has occurred in recent years

Figure 10-1. Examples of Public Health Strategies and the Frequency of Behavior Required by the Individual Being Protected.

Public Health Strategies

Frequency of Behavior Required by the Individual Being Protected	Active		Passive
	Persuasion	Law and Administrative Directives	
Never	logically impossible	logically impossible	pasteurization of milk, energy absorbing steering assemblies
Once	certain immunizations	immunizations to enter school	logically impossible
Once every few years	immunizations requiring boosters	immunizations to obtain certain visas	
Once per year	cervical cytology	physical examinations in certain organizations	
Biannually	dental checkups	variably periodic check-ups of workers handling certain hazardous materials	
Every few weeks	prenatal examinations		
Daily	vigorous exercise	exercise periods required of workers in certain industries in a few countries	
Each time the individual is protected	use of safety belts in most areas of the world	use of safety belts in a few countries	

181

with a commensurate decline in cases of cervical cancer spread beyond the original site of malignancy. Yet in a recently reported study, only slightly over half of the vulnerable population was found to have had at least one examination (Breslow, 1972). In the case of more frequently required behavior such as safety belt use and reduction of smoking, use rates are such that their consequences in damaged people are of epidemic proportions. This continues in spite of numerous mass media compaigns, the operation of all sorts of behavior modification clinics in the case of smoking, and the buzzer-light and interlock reminder systems in the case of safety belt use.

Passive strategies to ameliorate some of these problems could include, in the case of smoking, time dependent standards, analogous to automobile pollution standards, applied to smoking materials and filters to promote competition in the reduction of some of the known harmful constituents. In the case of motor vehicle injuries, there are well-known means of managing energy both within the vehicle structure (*e.g.*, cushions that inflate in a serious crash) and in the environment (*e.g.*, remove trees and other unnecessary objects from the roadside, make poles break away, or place energy-absorbing materials in front of them).

Passive strategies have received little consideration in the matter of the limitation of population size. This despite the fact that birth-control campaigns involving attempts at persuasion have met strong resistance in many areas because of historical and cultural factors that place a high value on large families, as well as concerns regarding the morality of preventing the initiation of human life. There is no way of knowing exactly what the reaction would be to a passive approach to population control. Such technology is not yet available. The technology, its proven safety, and the mechanism whereby it controlled one of the necessary conditions for pregnancy would no doubt affect its acceptance in particular cultures.

Implementing Strategies

The implementation of passive strategies may involve decisions in the form of voting on a community referendum (as fluoridation of water has in many jurisdictions) but more often involves legal or regulative mechanisms on the part of government and private corporate interests. The advantage is that the behavior of only a relatively few individuals or organizations must be regulated and monitored. The problem is one of changing these individuals and organizations.

As noted in our discussions of physicians in relation to patients and of the overall medical care system in Chapters 4 through 6, the present knowledge of medical care systems is minimal. There are few known factors that are readily manipulable. The federal government has attempted to change the system mainly by providing money for research, education, hospital construction, and payment for services for some groups in the population. These efforts have no doubt been beneficial in many respects, but they have also, in combination with other elements of the system, contributed to inefficiencies, waste, fragmentation of services, and inflation of costs to the point that many people without government assistance or adequate insurance cannot afford medical care. Others have little or no care available because of its uneven distribution.

Health insurance for all citizens had little chance of implementation until the 1970's. Large-scale governmental action in the equitable distribution of services is likely to be slow in developing, if it ever occurs, because of the free-enterprise ideology and the ability of groups that strongly hold to that ideology to influence governmental policy.

Continuous pressure from groups that are deprived of services because of inequity in the distribution of wealth or the geographic imbalance in the distribution of services is likely to lead to incentives to health professionals to practice in neglected areas and supplements to medical and other professional schools to increase the number of particular types of practitioners. The prospects for a governmentally organized and controlled national health service in the U.S. are slim unless a severe economic depression were to occur with accompanying large-scale shifts in ideology and organization of the relevant interest groups. However, some controls on costs and quality of care are beginning to accompany governmental financing.

The input of money at particular levels and echelons of the system can be a powerful tool in shifting the organization and process of the elements toward desired ends. However, these ends must be clearly discerned and the system must be well enough understood so that unintended consequences can be avoided. The infusion of money often creates bureaucracies and constituencies that become interested in their self-preservation rather than in solving the overall problems of the system.

For example, when federal money was available for the construction of hospitals, large numbers of hospitals were built, often by small communities which are finding 20 years later that they do not need hospital beds as much as they do ambulatory care facilities. The impact of the money for research has resulted in not only large amounts of basic research in university centers, but also in a shift in the emphasis of the professional medical educator from patient care and education to research. These educators, since their source of income has come from their research activities, have naturally tended to focus their attention on those matters, and the medical schools have become filled with physicians who present to the student a model of the physician interested in research in the laboratory rather than in the practice of medicine. As a result, increasing numbers of students have elected not to enter the part of the medical care system that delivers primary care but to remain in an institutional setting involved in medical research. As long as what seemed to be unlimited funds for research remained available, this trend continued until the system became grossly imbalanced.

It would be presumptuous to propose a utopian model for a medical care system in view of the present paucity of knowledge, but information already obtained suggests a few principles that may contribute to the amelioration of some current problems and the avoidance of future crises. Where passive strategies are unavailable, it appears that personalized medical care achieved through continuity of relationship of the patient with the physician is most likely to result in patient compliance with recommended health-related behavior. Such a relationship also results in more efficient use of facilities (hospitals and laboratories), and the patients, on average, report greater satisfaction with such care (Robertson, *et al.*, 1974). Thus, medical care organizations that will result in a discontinuous physician-patient relationship should be avoided.

The size of a medical care organization is also an important

184

factor in the outcome of medical care. Although an optimal size remains to be specified, it is clear that large bureaucracies tend to be associated with depersonalized medical care. Some elements of bureaucracy are inevitable where complex technology requiring large numbers of people is necessary. Hospitals under a certain size could not sustain such technology efficiently. Therefore, it would seem reasonable to send only those patients who need such technology to such hospitals, on some sort of regional basis.

The use of incentives, regulation, or whatever strategy to develop a given system and avoid unintended consequences requires periodic information about the consequences of the strategy and the use of that knowledge in adjusting the system. Again, this is the principle of feedback. Presently, there are some feedback systems in the form of health statistics and consumer complaints but the flow of this information to decision-makers is haphazard. It is theoretically possible to construct much more finely tuned feedback systems. In some labor union contracts, for example, wage increases are based on the cost of living index, a composite of the costs of goods and services issued periodically by the government. It should be possible to develop criteria for inexpensively measuring factors considered essential for good medical care, such as continuity and physician-patient ratios. A formula could then be devised that resulted in automatic adjustment of incentive payments or some other sanction to maintain the criteria in a desired range.

Ideally the criteria that one would like to monitor and control are outcome variables such as death, illness, and injury rates, rather than process variables. However, for such outcome variables to be comparable among medical care organizations, precise adjustments have to be made to account for differences in the kinds and severity of problems that the patients bring to the organization. For example, an Injury Severity Score has been developed that is strongly correlated with survival. Using such scores, medical care organizations can be compared on input of cases of relative severity and output in terms of survival (Baker, *et al.,* 1974). Similar research is needed for other types of human damage.

There is some pressure being exerted to increase quality and effectiveness of care. The Medicare legislation, as amended in 1972, required that by January, 1974, the medical profession organ-

185

ize itself into a series of Professional Standards Review Organizations (PSRO) to evaluate hospitalizations with respect to necessity of admission, length of stay, and quality of care.

While at this time the standards for the review of hospitalizations are being left in the hands of the physicians and the general theme of the legislation is to improve the quality of medical care in hospitals, the stick that goes with the carrot is that failure to comply with these regulations will result in no payment by the government for the hospitalization. It can be anticipated that this type of review mechanism will apply in time not only to patients covered under Medicare and Medicaid but also to those with other insurance benefits.

Once the review mechanism is developed for the delivery of hospital care, it seems certain that it will also be applied to the delivery of ambulatory care. This will be true particularly if insurance plans, sponsored either by the government or by the private sector, continue their trend toward more comprehensive coverage of medical care.

What these recent developments indicate is that feedback mechanisms are evolving through third-party payers of medical care either in the form of the government or the private insurance companies. These parties have at last become responsive to the rising cost of medical care and are seeking some method of changing the structure of the medical care system through the use of their economic power.

Given the phenomenal rise in costs of health care, this may be a necessary and beneficial development. However, these systems bear close watching because of the possibility that the minimization of costs will take priority over caring for the sick and injured. It is unusual in any complex system to be able to maximize (or minimize as the case may be) more than one outcome at a time. The physician who takes seriously his oath of maximum benefit to the patient will have difficulty with any attempt to reduce that benefit in the interest of reduced costs.

"Cost-effective" and "cost-benefit" are terms being thrown around in the debate over financing medical care. They should be carefully distinguished. A program is cost-effective if it achieves a goal at the least possible cost. Note that it is the goal that is maximized; the cost is minimized only after the goal is set.

However, many government and other health-related programs are being justified or abandoned on the basis of a ratio of benefits to costs (Brown, 1969; Merewitz and Sosnick, 1971).

To do a cost-benefit analysis, one must reduce potential benefits of programs to monetary terms. Thus, the worth of a governmental action in health-related areas is sometimes calculated on the basis of the estimated future earnings and tax-paying power of those to be protected from disease and injury. Carrying such thinking to its logical end, there would be no governmental programs for children born with congenital defects that result in their never becoming earners and taxpayers. The old who have no prospects for future productivity would be allowed to draw only on their contribution to and accrued interest from Social Security and left to otherwise fend for themselves.

Clearly, cost-benefit analysis has not been carried to its logical extreme in some government programs. But decisions based on cost-benefit ratios are being made in other programs that condemn some people to death or a lifetime of misery, while others live in luxury. For example, a proposed federal standard that would require truck manufacturers to put devices on the rear of trucks to prevent "underride" in rear-end crashes that often shear off the heads of car occupants was dropped because the National Highway Traffic Safety Administration claimed that "the safety benefits achievable in terms of lives and injuries saved would not be commensurate with the cost of implementing the proposed requirements" (Insurance Institute for Highway Safety, 1971).

In a society with limited resources, there is a point beyond which the cost of an effort is prohibitive, both in absolute terms and in terms of the use of resources for greater effectiveness in some other effort. However, many benefits are not reducible to dollars. Economists may argue over the dollar value of a human life, but each of us values his own life in other than monetary terms.

More knowledge of the structure and process of governmental and other organizations is needed in order to know how to make these organizations anticipate and respond to problems before they reach the crisis stage. Muckraking exposé has been partially effective but it occurs after the problem is acute, tends to be short-lived, and soon forgotten. Nevertheless, the politician looking for an issue and the investigative newspaper, magazine, or television re-

187

porter are potent allies for those seeking to change the policies of these organizations.

The permanence of the emerging consumer and citizen organizations that are developing intermittent or continuous monitoring of particular problems and of the actions of governmental and other organizations in resolving them is problematic. Organizations that must deal directly with human losses, such as insurance companies, are becoming more aware of the systems that contribute to those losses, and are becoming more active in exerting pressures toward amelioration of the problems.

Future research in medical sociology can do much to facilitate the feedback of information within and among organizations as to the extent of problems, the conditions necessary for their continuance, and the effectiveness of ameliorative strategies. The aspiring medical sociologist should be aware of the tools needed to analyze the systems involved. In addition to a basic curriculum in sociology, knowledge of biology, medicine, and mathematics is essential. Mistaken assumptions about and categorizations of data lead to poor research. Without knowledge of geometry, calculus, and mathematical statistics, the researcher will not be able to analyze data. If future medical sociologists gain such knowledge and collaborate with colleagues in relevant disciplines, we can expect exciting new discoveries and contributions to the field.

References

Abdellah, F. G. and Levine, E. Work sampling applied to the study of nursing personnel. *Nursing Research* 3:11–16, 1954.

Abel-Smith, B. *The Hospitals: 1800–1948.* London: Heineman, 1964.

Adams, R. Internal-mammary-artery ligation for coronary insufficiency. *New England Journal of Medicine* 258:113–115, 1958.

Adams, W. (ed.). *The Brain Drain.* New York: Macmillan, 1968.

AMA, Reference Data on *The Profile of Medical Practice,* 1972. Chicago: American Medical Association, 1972a.

AMA, *Socioeconomic Issues of Health,* 1972. Chicago: American Medical Association, 1972b.

Anderson, C. L. *Community Health.* St. Louis: C. V. Mosby Co., 1969.

Anderson, J. E. *The Emergence of the Modern Regulatory State.* Washington, D.C.: Public Affairs Press, 1962.

Anderson, J. G. Causal models and social indicators: toward the development of social systems models. *American Sociological Review* 38:285–301, 1973.

Anderson, O. W. *Health Care: Can There Be Equity? The United States, Sweden, and England.* New York: John Wiley and Sons, 1972.

REFERENCES

Andrews, J. L., Jr. Medical care in Sweden: lessons for America. *Journal of the American Medical Association* 223:1396, 1973.

Arieli, Y. *Individualism and Nationalism in American Ideology.* Cambridge: Harvard University Press, 1964.

Aronow, W. S. *et al.* Effect of freeway travel on angina pectoris. *Annals of Internal Medicine* 77: 669–676, 1972.

Badgely, R. F. and Wolfe, S. *Doctor's Strike: Medical Care and Conflict in Saskatchewan.* New York: Atherton Press, 1967.

Baker, S. P. Injury control. In Sartwell, P. E. (ed.), *Preventive Medicine and Public Health.* New York: Appleton-Century-Crofts, 1973.

Baker, S. P. *et al.* Fatal unintentional carbon monoxide poisoning in motor vehicles. *American Journal of Public Health* 62:1463–1467, 1972.

Baker, S. P.; O'Neill, B.; Haddon, W., Jr.; and Long, W. G. The injury severity score: a method for describing patients with multiple injuries and evaluating emergency care. *The Journal of Trauma* 14:187–196, 1974.

Bandura, A. and Walters, R. *Social Learning and Personality Development.* New York: Holt, Rinehart and Winston, 1963.

Banta, H. and Fox, C. Role strains of a health care team in a poverty community. *Social Science and Medicine* 6:697–722, 1972.

Beadle, G. and Beadle, M. *The Language of Life.* New York: Doubleday and Company, 1966.

Becker, H. S.; Geer, B.; Hughes, E. C.; and Strauss, A. L. *Boys in White.* Chicago: University of Chicago Press, 1961.

Becker, M. H.; Drachman, R. H.; and Kirscht, J. P. Motivations as predictors of health behavior. *Health Services Reports* 87:852–862, 1972a.

Becker, M. H.; Drachman, R. H.; and Kirscht, J. P. Predicting mother's compliance with pediatric medical regimen. *Journal of Pediatrics* 81:843–854, 1972b.

Becker, M. H.; Katatsky, M. E.; and Sidel, H. M. Unsuccessful medical school applicants as a potential health manpower resource. *Health Services Reports* 89:162–169, 1974.

Beecher, H. K. Quantitative effects of drugs on the mind. In Talalay, P. (ed.), *Drugs in Our Society.* Baltimore: The Johns Hopkins Press, 1964.

Beecher, H. K. The appraisal of analgesic agents in recent decades: prototypes for the study of subjective responses. In Blake,

J. B. (ed.), *Safeguarding the Public: Historical Aspects of Medicinal Drug Control.* Baltimore: The Johns Hopkins Press, 1970.

Bellin, L. E. *Realpolitik* in the health care arena: standard setting of professional services. *American Journal of Public Health* 59:820–825, 1971.

Bergman, A. B. and Werner, R. J. Failure of children to receive penicillin by mouth. *New England Journal of Medicine* 268:1334, 1963.

Berki, S. E. National health insurance: an idea whose time has come? *The Annals of the American Academy of Political and Social Science* 399: 125–144, 1972.

Berkowitz, L. Impulse, aggression and the gun. *Psychology Today* September: 18–22, 1968.

Berkowitz, L. *Roots of Aggression.* New York: Atherton Press, 1969.

Bernstein, M. H. Independent regulatory agencies: a perspective on their reform. *The Annals of the American Academy of Political and Social Science* 404:14–26, 1972.

Berrien, F. K. *General and Social Systems.* New Brunswick: Rutgers University Press, 1968.

Blackwell, B. The literature of delay in seeking medical care for chronic illnesses. *Health Education Monographs* 16:3–31, 1963.

Blau, P. M. and Scott, W. R. *Formal Organizations.* San Francisco: Chandler Publishing Company, 1962.

Blizzard, P. J. Beliefs about disease and alcoholism. *Mental Hygiene* 55:184–189, 1971.

Bloom, S. W. The sociology of medical education. *The Milbank Memorial Fund Quarterly* 43:174–184, 1965.

Bloom, S. W. The medical school as a social system: a case study of faculty-student relations. *The Milbank Memorial Fund Quarterly* XLIX:1–89, 1971.

Bogoch, S. *The Biochemistry of Memory.* New York: Oxford University Press, 1968.

Breslow, L. Early case-finding, treatment, and mortality from cervix and breast cancer. *Preventive Medicine* 1:141–152, 1972.

Brill, N. Q. and Storrow, H. C. Social class and psychiatry. *AMA Archives of General Psychiatry* 3:340–344, 1960.

Brockington, F. *World Health.* London: J. and A. Churchill, Ltd., 1967.

Brodsky, L. A biochemical survey of schizophrenia. *Canadian Psychiatric Association Journal* 15: 375–388, 1970.

REFERENCES

Brooks, H. *The Government of Science.* Cambridge: M.I.T. Press, 1968.

Brown, G. D. Planning for programming budgeting systems. In *Selected Papers on Systems for Health Care Delivery.* Iowa City, Iowa: University of Iowa Graduate Program in Hospital and Health Administration, 1969.

Brown, J. W.; Robertson, L. S.; Kosa, J.; and Alpert, J. J. A study of general practice in Massachusetts. *Journal of the American Medical Association* 216:301–306, 1971.

Bryant, J. *Health and the Developing World.* Ithaca, N.Y.: Cornell University Press, 1969.

Bucher, R. Social process and power in a medical school. In Zald, M. N. (ed.), *Power in Organizations.* Nashville, Tenn.: Vanderbilt University Press, 1970.

Buckley, W. *Sociology and Modern Systems Theory.* Englewood Cliffs, N.J.: Prentice-Hall, 1967.

Buckley, W. (ed.). *Modern Systems Research for the Behavioral Scientist.* Chicago: Aldine Publishing Co., 1968.

Burrow, J. G. The prescription-drug policies of the American Medical Association in the progressive era. In Blake, J. B. (ed.), *Safeguarding the Public: Historical Aspects of Medicinal Drug Control.* Baltimore: The Johns Hopkins Press, 1970.

Calder, R. *Medicine and Man.* New York: The New American Library of World Literature, 1958.

Campbell, I. R. and Mergard, E. G. *Aspects of Lead: An Annotated Bibliography.* Environmental Protection Agency Publication No. AP–104. Washington, D.C.: U.S. Government Printing Office, 1972.

Carey, W. D. Science policy making in the United States. In DeReuck, A. and Knight, J. (eds.), *Decision Making in National Science Policy.* Boston: Little, Brown and Company, 1968.

Cassel, J. Physical illness in response to stress. In Levine, S. and Scotch, N. A. (eds.), *Social Stress.* Chicago: Aldine Publishing Co., 1970.

Cavers, D. B. The evolution of the contemporary system of drug regulation under the 1938 act. In Blake, J. B. (ed.), *Safeguarding the Public: Historical Aspects of Medicinal Drug Control.* Baltimore: The Johns Hopkins Press, 1970.

Chabot, A. Improved infant mortality rates in a population served by a comprehensive health program. *Pediatrics* 47:989–994, 1971.

Charney, E. *et al.* How well do patients take oral penicillin? A collaborative study in private practice. *Pediatrics* 40:188–195, 1967.

Coe, R. M. *Sociology of Medicine.* New York: McGraw-Hill, 1970.

Coleman, J. S. *Community Conflict.* New York: The Free Press, 1957.

Coleman, J. S. *Introduction to Mathematical Sociology.* New York: The Free Press, 1964.

Coleman, J. S. *et al. Medical Innovation: A Diffusion Study.* Indianapolis: Bobbs-Merrill, 1966.

Conant, R. W. *The Politics of Community Health.* Washington, D.C.: Public Affairs Press, 1968.

Congressional Record. Motor vehicle and schoolbus safety amendments of 1974. August 12:H8119ff, 1974.

Congressional Record. Bill to revoke seatbelt interlock and buzzer. August 13:S14730ff, 1974.

Coombs, R. H. and Boyle, B. P. The transition to medical school: expectations versus realities. In Coombs, R. H. and Vincent, C. E. (eds.), *Psychosocial Aspects of Medical Training.* Springfield, Ill.: Charles C. Thomas, 1971.

Cooper, B. S. and McGee, M. F. Medical care outlays for three age groups; young, intermediate and aged. *Social Security Bulletin* 34:3–14, 1971.

Coopersmith, S. *The Antecedents of Self-Esteem.* San Francisco: W. H. Freeman and Co., 1967.

Crain, R. L.; Katz, E.; and Rosenthal, D. B. *The Politics of Community Conflict: The Fluoridation Decision.* Indianapolis: Bobbs-Merrill, 1969.

Croog, S. H. Ethnic origins, educational level, and response to a health questionnaire. *Human Organization* 20:65–69, 1961.

Daniels, A. K. Military psychiatry: the emergence of a subspecialty. In Friedson, E. and Lorber, J., *Medical Men and Their Work.* Chicago-New York: Aldine-Atherton, 1972.

Darley, W. and Somers, A. Medicine, money and manpower—the challenge to professional education: increasing personnel. *New England Journal of Medicine* 276:1414–1423, 1967.

Darwin, C. *The Expression of the Emotions in Man and Animals.* Chicago: University of Chicago Press, 1965.

Dodge, D. L. and Martin, W. T. *Social Stress and Chronic Illness.* Notre Dame, Ind.: University of Notre Dame Press, 1970.

Dohrenwend, B. S. and Dohrenwend, B. P. Stress situations,

birth order, and psychological symptoms. *Journal of Abnormal Psychology* 71: 215–223, 1966.

Dollard, J. *et al. Frustration and Aggression.* New Haven: Yale University Press, 1939.

Dowling, H. F. The American Medical Association policy on drugs in recent decades. In Blake, J. B. (ed.), *Safeguarding the Public: Historical Aspects of Medicinal Drug Control.* Baltimore: The Johns Hopkins Press, 1970.

Dubé, W. F. Applicants for the 1972–73 medical school entering class. *Journal of Medical Education* 48:1161–1163, 1973.

Dubé, W. F.; Johnson, D. G.; and Nelson, B. C. Study of U.S. medical school applicants, 1971–1972. *Journal of Medical Education* 48:395–420, 1973.

Dublin, T. D. The migration of physicians to the United States. *New England Journal of Medicine* 286:870–877, 1972.

Dubois, A. B. *et al. Effects of Chronic Exposure to Low Levels of Carbon Monoxide.* Washington, D.C.: National Academy of Sciences and National Academy of Engineering, 1968.

Duff, R. S. and Hollingshead, A. B. *Sickness and Society.* New York: Harper and Row, 1968.

Ehrlich, P. R. and Ehrlich, A. H. *Population, Resources, Environment.* San Francisco: W. H. Freeman and Co., 1972.

Eron, L. D. The effects of medical education on attitudes. *Journal of Medical Education* 30:559–566, 1955.

Fein, R. On achieving access and equity in health care. *Milbank Memorial Fund Quarterly* 50:157–190, 1972.

Field, M. G. *Soviet Socialized Medicine: An Introduction.* New York: The Free Press, 1967.

Fink, D.; Malloy, M. J.; Cohen, M. *et al.* Effective patient care in the pediatric ambulatory setting: a study of the acute care clinic. *Pediatrics* 43:927–935, 1969.

Flexner, A. *Medical Education in the United States and Canada.* New York: The Carnegie Foundation, 1910.

Foldvary, L. A. and Lane, J. C. The effect of compulsory wearing of seat-belts in Victoria. *Accident Analysis and Prevention,* in press.

Ford, A. B.; Liske, R. E.; Ort, R. S.; and Denton, J. C. *The Doctor's Perspective: Physicians View Their Patients and Practice.* Cleveland: The Press of Case Western Reserve University, 1967.

Fox, J. P. *et al. Epidemiology: Man and Disease.* New York: Macmillan, 1970.

Fox, R. C. Training for uncertainty. In Merton, R. K. et al. (eds.), *The Student Physician.* Cambridge: Harvard University Press, 1957.

Fox, R. C. *Experiment Perilous.* New York: The Free Press, 1959.

Frederiksen, H. Feedbacks in economic and demographic transition. *Science* 166:837–847, 1969.

French, D. Missing links in achieving effective health services. *Bulletin of the New York Academy of Medicine* 46:1129–1134, 1970.

Fried, M. Social differences in mental health. In Kosa, J. *et al.* (eds.), *Poverty and Health: A Sociological Analysis,* Cambridge: Harvard University Press, 1969.

Friedson, E. Client control and medical practice. *American Journal of Sociology* 65:374–382, 1960.

Fritschler, A. L. *Smoking and Politics: Policymaking and the Federal Bureaucracy.* New York: Appleton-Century-Crofts, 1969.

Fry, J. *Medicine in Three Societies.* Guildford and London: Billing and Sons, Ltd., 1969.

Fry, J. and Farndale, W. A. J. (eds.). *International Medical Care.* Oxford and Lancaster: Medical and Technical Publishing, 1972.

Funkenstein, D. H. The changing pool of medical school applicants, 1966–1967. *Journal of Medical Education* 43:1–13, 1968.

Funkenstein, D. H. Implications of the rapid social changes in university and medical schools for the education of future physicians. *Journal of Medical Education* 43:433–454, 1968.

Funkenstein, D. H. *et al. Mastery of Stress.* Cambridge: Harvard University Press, 1957.

Gardner, M. *Fads and Fallacies in the Name of Science.* New York: Dover Publications, 1957.

Geertsma, R. H. and Frinols, D. R. Specialty choice in medicine. *Journal of Medical Education* 47:509–517, 1972.

Geiger, H. J. The neighborhood health center. *Archives of Environmental Health* 14:912–916, 1967.

Goffman, E. *Stigma.* Englewood Cliffs, N.J.: Prentice-Hall, 1963.

Goldman, L. and Ebbert, A. The fate of medical student liberalism: a prediction. *Journal of Medical Education* 48:1095–1103, 1973.

Goldsen, R. K. Patient delay in seeking cancer diagnosis. *Journal of Chronic Diseases* 16:427–436, 1963.

Goodman, N. M. *International Health Organizations and Their*

Work. Philadelphia-New York: The Blakiston Company, 1952.

Gordon, G. *Role Theory and Illness*. New Haven: College and University Press, 1966.

Goss, M. E. W. Influence and authority among physicians in an outpatient clinic. *American Sociological Review* 26:30–50, 1961.

Green, L. W. *Status Identity and Preventive Health Behavior*. Pacific Health Education No. 1. Berkeley and Honolulu: University of California and University of Hawaii Schools of Public Health, 1970.

Haberman, P. W. The reliability and validity of the data. In Kosa, J.; Antonovsky, A.; and Zola, I. K. (eds.), *Poverty and Health*. Cambridge: Harvard University Press, 1969.

Hackett, T. P.; Cassem, N. H.; and Raker, J. W. Patient delay in cancer. *New England Journal of Medicine* 289:14–20, 1973.

Haddon, W., Jr. The changing approach to the epidemiology, prevention, and amelioration of trauma; the transition to approaches etiologically rather than descriptively based. *American Journal of Public Health* 58:1431–1438, 1968.

Haddon, W., Jr. On the escape of tigers: an ecologic note (editorial). *American Journal of Public Health* 60:2229–2234, 1970.

Haddon, W., Jr. Road safety problems and action programs—the U.S. approach. National Road Safety Symposium, Canberra, Australia, 1972.

Haddon, W., Jr. and Goddard, J. L. An analysis of highway safety strategies. In *Passenger Car Design and Highway Safety*. New York: Association for the Aid of Crippled Children and Consumers Union of the U.S., 1962.

Haddon, W., Jr.; Suchman, E. A.; and Klein, D. (eds.). *Accident Research*. New York: Harper and Row, 1964.

Haefner, D. P. *et al.* Preventive actions in dental disease, tuberculosis, and cancer. *Public Health Reports* 82:451–459, 1967.

Haefner, D. P. and Kirscht, J. P. Motivational and behavioral effects of modifying health beliefs. *Public Health Reports* 85:478–484, 1970.

Haggerty, R. J. Etiology of the decline in general practice. *Journal of the American Medical Association* 185:109–112, 1963.

Haire, M. (ed.). *Modern Organization Theory*. New York: John Wiley and Sons, 1959.

Hall, A. D. and Fagen, R. E. Definition of system. *General Systems* 1:18–28, 1956.

Hallman, H. W. *Neighborhood Control of Public Programs:*

Case Studies of Community Corporations and Neighborhood Boards. New York: Praeger Publishers, 1970.

Hardin, G. The tragedy of the commons. *Science* 162:1243–1248, 1968.

Hardin, G. *Exploring New Ethics for Survival.* Baltimore: Penguin Books, 1973.

Hare, E. H. and Shaw, G. K. A study in family health: (1) health in relation to family size. *British Journal of Psychiatry* 11:461–466, 1965.

Harnish, T. I. Regional medical program planning. *American Journal of Public Health* 59:770–772, 1969.

Harris, S. E. *The Economics of American Medicine.* New York: Macmillan, 1964.

Hartung, R. and Dinman, B. D. (eds.). *Environmental Mercury Contamination.* Ann Arbor: Ann Arbor Science Publishers, 1972.

Hassall, C. and Trethowan, W. H. Suicide in Birmingham. *British Medical Journal* 1:717–718, 1972.

Hawley, W. D. and Wirt, F. M. *The Search for Community Power.* Englewood Cliffs, N.J.: Prentice-Hall, 1968.

Heagarty, M. C. and Robertson, L. S. Slave doctors and free doctors—a participant observer study of the physician-patient relation in a low-income comprehensive-care program. *The New England Journal of Medicine* 284:636–641, 1971.

Henderson, J. G. Denial and repression as factors in the delay of patients with cancer presenting themselves to the physician. *Annals of the New York Academy of Science* 125:856–864, 1966.

Heston, L. The genetics of schizophrenia and schizoid disease. *Science* 167:249–256, 1970.

Hirakis, S. S. *et al.* Statewide fluoridation: how it was done in Connecticut. *Journal of the American Dental Association* 75:174–178, 1967.

Hirst, L. F. *The Conquest of Plague: A Study of the Evolution of Epidemiology.* Oxford: Clarendon Press, 1953.

Hochheiser, L. I.; Woodward, K.; and Charney, E. Effect of the neighborhood health center on the use of pediatric emergency departments in Rochester, N.Y. *New England Journal of Medicine* 285:148–152, 1971.

Hollingshead, A. B. and Redlich, F. C. *Social Class and Mental Illness.* New York: John Wiley and Sons, 1958.

Holmes, T. H. and Masuda, M. Life changes and illness suceptibility. Symposium on Separation and Depression, Annual Meeting of the American Association for the Advancement of Science, Chicago, Ill., December 26–30, 1970.

Holmes, T. H. and Rahe, R. H. The social readjustment scale. *Journal of Psychosomatic Research* 11:213, 1967.

Hunter, D. *The Diseases of Occupations.* London: English Universities Press, 1969.

Immunization Survey—United States, 1971. *Morbidity and Mortality* 20:435–437, 1971.

Insurance Institute for Highway Safety. DOT scraps 'underride' proposal. *Status Report* 6:(13)1–2.

Jackson, C. L. and Carpenter, L. Effect of a state law intended to require immunization of school children. *Health Services Reports* 87:461–466, 1972.

Jackson, C. O. *Food and Drug Legislation in the New Deal.* Princeton: Princeton University Press, 1970.

Jackson, E. F. Status consistency and symptoms of stress. *American Sociological Review* 27:469–480, 1962.

Jackson, E. F. and Burke, P. J. Status and symptoms of stress: additive and interactive effects. *American Sociological Review* 30: 556–564, 1965.

Jaco, E. G. Mental illness in response to stress. In Levine, S. and Scotch, N. A. (eds.), *Social Stress.* Chicago: Aldine Publishing Co., 1970.

Jenkins, C. D. Group differences in perception: a study of community beliefs and feelings about tuberculosis. *The American Journal of Sociology* 71:417–429, 1966.

Kadushin, C. *Why People Go to Psychiatrists.* New York: Atherton Press, 1969.

Kasl, S. V. *et al.* Serum uric acid and cholesterol in achievement behavior and motivation. *Journal of the American Medical Association* 213:1158–1165, 1291–1300, 1970.

Kasl, S. V. and Cobb, S. Health behavior, illness behavior, and sick role behavior. *Archives of Environmental Health* 12:246–266, 1966.

Katz, J. *Experimentation with Human Beings.* New York: Russell Sage Foundation, 1972.

Kegeles, S. S. A field experimental attempt to change beliefs and behavior of women in an urban ghetto. *Journal of Health and Social Behavior* 10:115–124, 1969.

Kegeles, S. S. *et al.* Survey of beliefs about cancer detection and taking Papanicolaou tests. *Public Health Reports* 80:815–823, 1964.

198

Kelley, A. B. *The Pavers and the Paved.* New York: Donald W. Brown, Inc., 1971.

Keyfitz, N. and Flieger, W. *World Population: An Analysis of Vital Data.* Chicago: University of Chicago Press, 1968.

King, S. H. *Perceptions of Illness and Medical Practice.* New York: Russell Sage Foundation, 1962.

Kirscht, J. P. *et al.* A national study of health beliefs. *Journal of Health and Social Behavior* 7:248–254, 1966.

Klein, M.; Roghmann, K.; Woodward, K.; and Charney, E. The impact of the Rochester neighborhood health center on hospitalization of children, 1968 to 1970. *Pediatrics* 51:833–839, 1973.

Koos, E. L. *The Health of Regionville.* New York: Columbia University Press, 1954.

Korman, M.; Stubblefield, R. L.; and Martin, L. W. Patterns of success in medical school and their correlates. *Journal of Medical Education* 43:405–411, 1968.

Korsch, B. M.; Gozzi, E. K.; and Francis, W. Gaps in doctor-patient communication. *Pediatrics* 42:855–871, 1968.

Kosa, J.; Antonovsky, A.; and Zola, I. K. (eds.). *Poverty and Health: A Sociological Analysis.* Cambridge: Harvard University Press, 1969.

Kosa, J. and Robertson, L. S. Social aspects of health and illness. In Kosa, J. *et al.* (eds.), *Poverty and Health: A Sociological Analysis.* Cambridge: Harvard University Press, 1969.

Kreuz, L. E. and Rose, R. M. Assessment of aggressive behavior and plasma testosterone in a young criminal population. *Psychosomatic Medicine* 34:321–332, 1972.

Kritzer, H. and Zimet, C. N. A retrospective view of medical specialty choice. *Journal of Medical Education* 42:47–53, 1967.

Kübler-Ross, E. *On Death and Dying.* New York: Macmillan, 1970.

Kutner, B. *et al.* Delay in the diagnosis and treatment of cancer: a critical analysis of the literature. *Journal of Chronic Diseases* 7:95–120, 1958.

Lambertson, E. Evaluating the quality of nursing care: Hospitals. *Journal of the American Hospital Association* 67:2129, 1967.

Langner, T. S. and Michael, S. T. *Life Stress and Mental Health.* New York: The Free Press, 1963.

Lasagna, L. 1938–1968: the FDA, the drug industry, the medical profession and the public. In Blake, J. B. (ed.), *Safeguarding the Public: Historical Aspects of Medicinal Drug Control.* Baltimore: The Johns Hopkins Press, 1970.

Lazarus, R. S. *Psychological Stress and the Coping Process.* New York: McGraw Hill, 1966.

Lehr, I.; Messinger, B.; and Rosenman, R. H. A sociobiological approach to the study of coronary heart disease. *Journal of Chronic Disease* 26:13–30, 1973.

Leone, R. C. Public interest advocacy and the regulatory process. *The Annals of the American Academy of Political and Social Science* 400:14–26, 1972.

Lerner, M. Social differences in physical health. In Kosa, J. *et al.* (eds.), *Poverty and Health: A Sociological Analysis.* Cambridge: Harvard University Press, 1969.

Le Shan, L. An emotional life history pattern associated with neoplastic disease. *Annals of the New York Academy of Sciences* 125:780–793, 1966.

Levine, G. N. Anxiety about illness: psychological and social bases. *Journal of Health and Human Behavior* 3:30–34, 1962.

Levine S. and Scotch, N. A. *Social Stress.* Chicago: Aldine Publishing Co., 1970.

Lewis, B. J. *VA Medical Program in Relation to Medical Schools.* Committee Print, House Committee on Veteran's Affairs. Washington, D.C.: U.S. Government Printing Office, 1970.

Liang, M. H.; Eichling, P. S.; Fine, L. J.; and Annas, G. J. Chinese health care: determinants of the system. *American Journal of Public Health* 63:102–110, 1973.

Lindemann, E. Symptomatology and management of acute grief. *American Journal of Psychiatry* 101:141–148, 1944.

Lindsey, A. *Socialized Medicine in England and Wales: The National Health Service, 1948–1961.* Chapel Hill: University of North Carolina Press, 1962.

Lord, W. *A Night to Remember.* New York: Henry Holt, 1955.

Lowi, T. J. American business, public policy, case-studies, and political theory. *World Politics* 16:677–715, 1964.

Lowry, R. P. *Who's Running This Town?: Community Leadership and Social Change.* New York: Harper and Row, 1962.

Lyden, F. H.; Geiger, H. G.; and Peterson, O. L. *The Training of Good Physicians: Critical Factors in Career Choices.* Cambridge: Harvard University Press, 1968.

MacLeod, G. K. and Prussin, J. A. The continuing evolution of health maintenance organizations. *New England Journal of Medicine* 288:439–443, 1973.

McCarry, C. *Citizen Nader,* New York: Saturday Review Press, 1972.

McDonald, A. P., Jr. Anxiety, Affiliation, and social isolation. *Development Psychology* 3:242–254, 1970.

McFadden, C. J. *Medical Ethics.* Philadelphia: F. A. Davis Company, 1967.

McKinlay, J. B. Some approaches and problems in the study of the use of services. *Journal of Health and Social Behavior* 13:115–152, 1972.

McNamara, M. E. and Todd, C. A. A survey of group practice in the United States, 1969. *American Journal of Public Health* 60:1303–1313, 1970.

McNeil, D. R. *The Fights for Flouridation.* New York: Oxford University Press, 1957.

Marmor, T. R. *The Politics of Medicare.* London: Routledge and Kegan Paul, 1970.

Maruyama, M. The second cybernetics: deviation—amplifying mutual causal processes. *American Scientist* 51:164–179, 1963.

Mason, J. W. "Over-all" hormonal balance as a key to endocrine research. *Psychosomatic Medicine* 30:791–808, 1968.

Masuda, M. and Holmes, T. H. Magnitude estimation of social readjustments. *Journal of Psychosomatic Research* 11:219, 1967.

Mazur, A. and Robertson, L. S. *Biology and Social Behavior.* New York: The Free Press, 1972.

Mechanic, D. The concept of illness behavior. *Journal of Chronic Diseases* 15:189–194, 1962.

Mechanic, D. and Volkart, E. H. Illness behavior and medical diagnoses. *Journal of Health and Human Behavior* 1:86–94, 1960.

Merewitz, L. and Sosnick, S. H. *The Budget's New Clothes.* Chicago: Markham Publishing Company, 1971.

Merton, R. K.; Reader, G. G.; and Kendall, P. L. *The Student Physician.* Cambridge: Harvard University Press, 1957.

Meyer, R. J. and Haggerty, R. J. Streptococcal infections in families: factors altering individual susceptibility. *Pediatrics* 29: 539–549, 1962.

Migeon, C. J. *et al.* The transplacental passage of various steroid hormones in mid-pregnancy. *Recent Progress in Hormone Research* 17:207–248, 1961.

Milgram, S. Behavioral study of obedience. *Journal of Abnormal and Social Psychology* 65:371–378, 1963.

Miller, J. G. The nature of living systems. *Behavioral Science* 16:277–301, 1971.

Miller, N. E. Learning of visceral and glandular responses. *Science* 163:434–445, 1969.

201

Miller, S. J. *Prescription for Leadership: Training for the Medical Elite.* Chicago: Aldine Publishing Co., 1970.

Mishler, E. G. and Waxler, N. E. Family interaction processes and schizophrenia: a review of current theories. *The Merrill-Palmer Quarterly of Behavior and Development* 11:269–315, 1965.

Moore, G. T.; Bernstein, R.; and Bonanno, R. A. Effect of a neighborhood health center on hospital emergency room use. *Medical Care* 10:240–247, 1972.

Muller, J. E.; Abdellah, F. G.; Billings, F. T.; Hess, A. E.; Petit, D.; and Egeberg, R. O. The Soviet health system—aspects of relevance for medicine in the United States. *New England Journal of Medicine* 286:693–702, 1972.

Mumford, E. *Interns: From Students to Physicians.* Cambridge: Harvard University Press, 1970.

National Academy of Sciences. *Air Quality and Automobile Emission Control.* Washington, D.C.: U.S. Government Printing Office, 1974.

Oates, R. P. and Feldman, H. H. Patterns of change in medical student career choices. *Journal of Medical Education* 49:562–569, 1974.

Olmstead, A. G. Bases of attraction to medicine and learning style preferences of medical students. *Journal of Medical Education* 48:572–576, 1973.

Otolorin, M. P. Priorities in medical services. In Prywes, M. and Davies, A. M. (eds.), *Health Problems in Developing States.* New York: Grune and Stratton, Inc., 1968.

Parks, R. B. *Community Health Services for New York City: A Case Study.* New York: Praeger Publishers, 1968.

Parry, J. *The Psychology of Human Communication.* London: University of London Press, 1968.

Parsons, T. *The Social System.* New York: The Free Press, 1951.

Perel, M. and Ziegler, P. M. An evaluation of a safety belt interlock system. Washington, D.C.: National Highway Traffic Safety Administration, 1971.

Perricone, P. J. Social concern in medical students: a reconsideration of the Eron assumption. *Journal of Medical Education* 49: 541–546, 1974.

Perrow, C. Hospitals: technology, structure and goals. In March, J. G., *Handbook of Organizations.* Chicago: Rand McNally and Company, 1965.

Persky, H. *et al.* Relation of psychologic measures of aggression and hostility to testosterone production in man. *Psychosomatic Medicine* 33:265–277, 1971.

Peterson, O. L.; Andrews, L. P.; Spain, R. S.; and Greenberg, B. G. An analytical study of North Carolina General Practice. *Journal of Medical Education* 31: Part 2, December, 1956.

Pinard, M. Structural attachments and political support in urban politics: the case of fluoridation referendums. *American Journal of Sociology* 68:513–526, 1963.

Plato. *The Dialogues of Plato, Laws, Book IV*. Translated by Jowett, B. New York: Random House, 1937.

Price, J. L. *Organizational Effectiveness: An Inventory of Propositions*. Homewood, Ill.: Richard D. Irwin, Inc., 1968.

Rayack, E. *Professional Power and American Medicine: The Economics of the American Medical Association*. Cleveland and New York: World Publishing Co., 1967.

Reinhardt, A. M. and Gray, R. M. A social psychological study of attitude change in physicians. *Journal of Medical Education* 47:112–117, 1973.

Rice, D. P. and Cooper, B. S. National health expenditures, 1929–71. *Social Security Bulletin* 35:3–18, 1972.

Riesman, D. *et al. The Lonely Crowd*. New Haven: Yale University Press, 1950.

Rifkin, S. P. Health care for rural areas. In Quinn, J. R. (ed.), *Medicine and Public Health in the Peoples Republic of China*. U.S. Public Health Service, DHEW Publication No. (NIH) 73–67. Washington, D.C.: U.S. Government Printing Office, 1973.

Roback, G. A. Physician manpower, 1970. In Balfe, B. E., *et al.* (eds.), *Reference Data on the Profile of Medical Practice*. Chicago: American Medical Association, 1971.

Robertson, L. S. Sociology stretches its goals (letter). *Science* 160:375–376, 1968.

Robertson, L. S. Safety belt use in automobiles with starter-interlock and buzzer-light reminder systems. Washington, D.C.: Insurance Institute for Highway Safety, 1974.

Robertson, L. S. *et al.* Family size and the use of medical resources. In Liu, W. T. (ed.), *Family and Fertility,* Notre Dame, Ind.: University of Notre Dame Press, 1967.

Robertson, L. S. *et al.* A controlled study of the effect of television messages on safety belt use. *American Journal of Public Health,* in press, 1974.

Robertson, L. S. and Dotson, L. E. Perceived parental expressivity, reaction to stress, and affiliation. *Journal of Personality and Social Psychology* 12: 229–234, 1969.

Robertson, L. S. and Haddon, W., Jr. The buzzer-light reminder system and safety belt use. *American Journal of Public Health* 64:814–815, 1974.

Robertson, L. S.; Kosa, J.; Heagarty, M. C.; Haggerty, R. J.; and Alpert, J. J. *Changing the Medical Care System: A Controlled Experiment in Comprehensive Care.* New York: Praeger Publishers, 1974.

Robertson, L. S.; O'Neill, B.; and Wixom, C. W. Factors associated with observed safety belt use. *Journal of Health and Social Behavior* 13:18–24, 1972.

Roemer, M. I. and Friedman, J. W. *Doctors in Hospitals: Medical Staff Organization and Hospital Performance.* Baltimore: The Johns Hopkins Press, 1971.

Roemer, M. I.; Mera, J. A.; and Shonick, W. The ecology of group practice in the United States. *Medical Care* 12:627–637, 1974.

Rogers, E. S. Public health asks of sociology. *Science* 159:506–508, 1968.

Rosenberg, M. *Society and the Adolescent Self-Image.* Princeton: Princeton University Press, 1965.

Rosenblueth, A. *et al.* Behavior, purpose, and teleology. *Philosophy of Science* 10:18–24, 1943.

Rosenblueth, A. and Wiener, N. Purposeful and non-purposeful behavior. *Philosophy of Science* 17:318–326, 1950.

Rosinori, E. Social class of medical students. *Journal of the American Medical Association* 193:95–98, 1965.

Ross, H. L. Law, science, and accidents: the British Road Safety Act of 1967. *The Journal of Legal Studies* 2:1–78, 1973.

Roy, D. F. Quota restriction and goldbricking in a machine shop. *American Journal of Sociology* 62:427–442, 1952.

Rutstein, D. C. *The Coming Revolution in Medicine.* Cambridge: M.I.T. Press, 1967.

Sachar, E. J. Psychological factors relating to activation and inhibition of the adrenocortical stress response in man: a review. *Progress in Brain Research* 32:316–324, 1970.

Sanazaro, P. J. Research in medical education: exploratory analysis of a black box. *Annals of the New York Academy of Sciences* 128:519–531, 1965.

Sapolsky, H. M. Science, voters and the fluoridation controversy. *Science* 162:427–433, 1968.

204

Schachter, S. *The Psychology of Affiliation.* Stanford: Stanford University Press, 1959.

Schaffer, A. and Schaffer, R. C. *Woodruff: A Study of Community Decision Making.* Chapel Hill: University of North Carolina Press, 1970.

Sears, R. *et al.* The socialization of aggression. In Maccoby, E. *et al.* (eds.), *Readings in Social Psychology.* New York: Holt, Rinehart and Winston, 1958.

Selye, H. *The Physiology and Pathology of Exposure to Stress.* Montreal: Acta, Inc., 1950.

Selye, H. *Calciphylaxis.* Chicago: University of Chicago Press, 1962.

Selye, H. *From Dream to Discovery.* New York: McGraw-Hill, 1964.

Selye, H. *Anaphylactoid Edema.* St. Louis: W. H. Green, 1968.

Selye, H. *Experimental Cardiovascular Diseases.* Heidelberg, Germany: Springer-Verlag, 1970.

Seward, E. W. The relevance of prepaid group practice to the effective delivery of health services. Presented at the 18th Annual Group Health Institute. Sault Ste. Marie, Ontario, Canada, June 18, 1969.

Shaw, D. J. Interim results from test drive I advanced features study. Transmitted to Docket 69–7, National Highway Traffic Safety Administration, July 27, 1971.

Shaw, G. B. *The Doctor's Dilemma: A Tragedy.* Harmondsworth: Middlesex, England: Penguin Books, Ltd., 1966.

Shenkin, B. N. Politics and medical care in Sweden: the seven crowns reform. *New England Journal of Medicine* 288:555–559, 1973.

Sheps, C. G. and Seipp, C. The medical school, its products and its problems. *The Annals of the American Academy of Political and Social Science* 399:38–49, 1972.

Sidel, V. W. Medical personnel and their training. In Quinn, J. R. (ed.), *Medicine and Public Health in the Peoples Republic of China.* U.S. Public Health Service, DHEW Publication No. (NIH) 73–67, Washington, D.C. U.S. Government Printing Office, 1973.

Sigerist, H. E. *American Medicine.* New York: W. W. Norton and Company, Inc., 1934.

Sigerist, H. E. The development of hospitals. In Roemer, M. I. (ed.), *On the Sociology of Medicine.* New York: MD Publications, 1960.

205

Silverman, M. and Lee, P. R. *Pills, Profits and Politics.* Berkeley: University of California Press, 1974.

Simmons, H. E. *The Psychogenic Theory of Disease.* Sacramento: Citadel Press, 1966.

Snyder, S. H. *et al.* Drugs, neurotransmitters, and schizophrenia. *Science* 184:1243–1253, 1974.

Solnit, A. Psychologic considerations in the management of deaths on pediatric hospital service. *Pediatrics* 24:106–112, 1959.

Sonnedecker, G. Contribution of the pharmaceutical profession toward controlling the quality of drugs in the nineteenth century. In Blake, J. B. (ed.), *Safeguarding the Public: Historical Aspects of Medicinal Drug Control.* Baltimore: The Johns Hopkins Press, 1970.

Source Book of Health Insurance Data. New York: Health Insurance Institute, 1970.

Srole, L. *et al. Mental Health in the Metropolis.* New York: McGraw-Hill, 1962.

Starfield, B. Health services research: a working model. *New England Journal of Medicine* 289:132–136, 1973.

Stebbins, E. L. Foreword. In Lilienfeld, A. M. and Gifford, A. J., *Chronic Diseases and Public Health.* Baltimore: The Johns Hopkins Press, 1966.

Steele, J. L. and McBroom, W. H. Conceptual and empirical dimensions of health behavior. *Journal of Health and Social Behavior* 13:382–392, 1974.

Stevens, R. and Stevens, R. Medicaid, anatomy of a dilemma. *Law and Contemporary Problems,* Spring, 1970.

Stoeckle, J. D. The future of health care. In Kosa, J. *et al.* (eds.), *Poverty and Health: A Sociological Analysis.* Cambridge: Harvard University Press, 1969.

Strickland, S. P. Integration of medical research and health policies. *Science* 173:1093–1103, 1971.

Suchman, E. A. Stages of illness and medical care. *Journal of Health and Human Behavior* 6:114–128, 1965a.

Suchman, E. A. Social patterns of illness and medical care. *Journal of Health and Human Behavior* 6:2–16, 1965b.

Susser, M. and Watson, W. *Sociology in Medicine.* New York: Oxford University Press, 1971.

Taylor, M.; Dickman, W.; and Kane, R. Medical students' attitudes toward family practice. *Journal of Medical Education* 48:885–895, 1973.

Taylor, R. Comments on a mechanistic conception of purposefulness. *Philosophy of Science* 17:310–317, 1950.

Titmuss, R. M. *The Gift Relationship: From Human Blood to Social Policy.* New York: Pantheon Books, 1971.

Twaddle, A. C. Health decisions and sick role variations: an exploration. *Journal of Health and Social Behavior* 10:105–115, 1969.

U.S. Department of Health, Education and Welfare. *The Health Consequences of Smoking.* Washington, D.C.: U.S. Government Printing Office, 1971.

Waddington, I. The role of the hospital and the development of modern medicine: a sociological analysis. *Sociology* 7:211–224, 1973.

Wardwell, W. I. Limited, marginal and quasi-practitioners. In Freeman, H. E.; Levine, S.; and Reeder, L. G. (eds.), *Handbook of Medical Sociology* (second edition). Englewood Cliffs, N.J.: Prentice-Hall, 1972.

Weber, M. *The Theory of Social and Economic Organizations.* Translated by Henderson, A. M. and Parsons, T. Glencoe: The Free Press, 1947.

Weinberger, H. L. and Richmond, H. B. Program implications of new knowledge regarding the physical, intellectual and emotional growth and development and the unmet needs of children and youth. *American Journal of Public Health* 60: Supplement, 1970.

Weinstein, R. M. Patient's perceptions of mental illness: paradigms for analysis. *Journal of Health and Social Behavior* 13:38–47, 1972.

Westman, W. E. and Gifford, R. M. Environmental impact: controlling the overall level. *Science* 181:819–825, 1973.

Wildavsky, A. *Leadership in a Small Town.* Totoway, N.J.: The Bedminster Press, 1964.

Williams, A. F. and Wechsler, H. Dimensions of preventive behavior. *Journal of Consulting and Clinical Psychology* 40:420–425, 1973.

Williams, R. C. *The United States Public Health Service 1798–1950.* Commissioned Officers Association of the United States Public Health Service. Washington, D.C., 1951.

Wooldridge, D. E. *et al. Biomedical Science and Its Administration: A Study of the National Institutes of Health.* Washington, D.C.: U.S. Government Printing Office, 1965.

Wyler, A. R. *et al.* Magnitude of life events and seriousness of illness. *Psychosomatic Medicine* 33:115–122, 1971.

Young, J. H. Drugs and the 1906 law. In Blake, J. B. (ed.), *Safeguarding the Public: Historical Aspects of Medicinal Drug Control.* Baltimore: The John Hopkins Press, 1970.

REFERENCES

Zbrowski, M. *People in Pain.* San Francisco: Jossey-Bass, Inc., 1969.

Zola, I. K. Culture and symptoms. *American Sociological Review* 31:615–630, 1966.

Name index

Abdellah, F. G., 115, 189, 202
Abel-Smith, B., 159–60, 189
Adams, R., 52, 189
Adams, S. H., 148
Adams, W., 164, 189
Alpert, J. J., 192, 204
Anderson, C. L., 128, 132, 140, 189
Anderson, J. E., 142, 189
Anderson, J. G., 54, 189
Anderson, O. W., 158–59, 189
Andrews, J. L., 162, 190
Andrews, L. P., 202
Annas, G. J., 200
Antonovsky, A., 199
Arieli, Y., 128, 190
Aronow, W. S., 25, 190

Badgely, R. F., 117, 190
Baker, S. P., 25, 180, 185, 190
Bandura, A., 10, 190
Banta, H., 88, 190
Beadle, G., 13, 190
Beadle, M., 13, 190
Becker, H. S., 78, 190
Becker, M. H., 69, 94–95, 190

Beecher, H. K., 51, 190–91
Bellin, L. E., 138, 191
Bergman, A. B., 95, 191
Berki, S. E., 146, 191
Berkowitz, L., 10, 191
Bernstein, M. H., 151, 191
Bernstein, R., 202
Berrien, F. K., 12, 191
Billings, F. T., 202
Blackwell, B., 57–58, 191
Blau, P. M., 61, 111, 191
Blizzard, P. J., 60, 191
Bloom, S. W., 73, 78, 191
Bogoch, S., 13, 191
Bonanno, R., 202
Boyle, B. P., 78, 193
Breslow, L., 182, 191
Brill, N. Q., 88, 191
Brockington, F., 166–67, 191
Brodsky, L., 41, 191
Brooks, H., 152, 192
Brown, G. D., 187, 192
Brown, J. W., 90, 192
Bryant, J., 162–63, 192
Bucher, R., 113, 192

209

Subject index

215

SUBJECT INDEX